Practical Docker with Python

Build, Release, and Distribute Your Python App with Docker

Second Edition

Sathyajith Bhat

Apress®

Practical Docker with Python: Build, Release, and Distribute Your Python App with Docker

Sathyajith Bhat
Bangalore, Karnataka, India

ISBN-13 (pbk): 978-1-4842-7814-7   ISBN-13 (electronic): 978-1-4842-7815-4
https://doi.org/10.1007/978-1-4842-7815-4

Managing Director, Apress Media LLC: Welmoed Spahr
Acquisitions Editor: Celestin Suresh John
Development Editor: James Markham
Coordinating Editor: Divya Modi
Copyeditor: Kezia Endsley

Cover designed by eStudioCalamar

Cover image designed by Pixabay

Distributed to the book trade worldwide by Springer Science+Business Media New York, 1 New York Plaza, New York, NY 10004. Phone 1-800-SPRINGER, fax (201) 348-4505, e-mail orders-ny@springer-sbm.com, or visit www.springeronline.com. Apress Media, LLC is a California LLC and the sole member (owner) is Springer Science + Business Media Finance Inc (SSBM Finance Inc). SSBM Finance Inc is a **Delaware** corporation.

For information on translations, please e-mail booktranslations@springernature.com; for reprint, paperback, or audio rights, please e-mail bookpermissions@springernature.com.

Apress titles may be purchased in bulk for academic, corporate, or promotional use. eBook versions and licenses are also available for most titles. For more information, reference our Print and eBook Bulk Sales web page at http://www.apress.com/bulk-sales.

Any source code or other supplementary material referenced by the author in this book is available to readers on GitHub via the book's product page, located at www.apress.com/9781484278147. For more detailed information, please visit http://www.apress.com/source-code.

Printed on acid-free paper

To my parents, Jyothika and Jayakar Bhat U., who have unconditionally supported me through my entire life.

Table of Contents

About the Author

 **Sathyajith Bhat** is a seasoned DevOps/SRE and Cloud Engineering professional currently working as a Site Reliability Engineer at Adobe. Prior to this, he introduced DevOps practices at Styletag.com.

Sathyajith is one of the organizers of the AWS User Group Bengaluru and has been recognized as an AWS Community Hero for his contributions to the AWS Community. He is also a volunteer Community Moderator at Super User and Web Apps Stack Exchange and occasionally livestreams gaming and coding on Twitch at twitch.tv/sathyabhat.

Sathyajith can be reached from these links:

Twitter: https://twitter.com/sathyabhat
LinkedIn: https://linkedin.com/in/sathyabhat
Email: contact@sathyasays.com

About the Technical Reviewer

Sourav Bhattacharjee currently works as a Senior Engineer with Oracle Cloud Infrastructure. He earned his master's degree from the Indian Institute of Technology, Kharagpur, India. Previously he worked with IBM Watson Health Lab. He has developed many scalable systems, published research papers, and has a few patents under his name. He is passionate about building large-scale systems and machine learning solutions.

Acknowledgments

Thank you to my wife, Jyothsna, for being patient and for supporting me in my career and while writing this book.

I would like to thank Celestin Suresh John, James Markham, and Divya Modi from Apress for helping me immensely through all the stages of this book.

I would like to thank my technical reviewer, Sourav Bhattacharjee, for his constructive suggestions and pertinent feedback.

Last but not least, I would like to acknowledge the immense support provided by Saurabh Minni, Ninad Pundalik, Prashanth H N, Ashwin Murali, Varun Sabari, Mrityunjay Iyer, and Abhijith Gopal over the past few years.

Introduction

Docker has exploded in popularity and has become the de facto target as a containerization image format and a containerization runtime. With modern applications getting more and more complicated, the increased focus on microservices has led to the adoption of Docker. It allows for applications, along with their dependencies, to be packaged into files as a container that can run on any system. This results in faster turnaround times in application deployment and less complexity. It all but negates the chances of the "it-works-on-my-server-but-not-on-yours" problem.

Practical Docker with Python covers the fundamentals of containerization, gets you acquainted with Docker, breaks down terminology like Dockerfiles and Docker volumes, and takes you on a guided tour of building a telegram bot using Python and containerizing the application. This second edition builds on the foundation of the first, with code updates and new examples that bring it up to date with the changes in Docker; it also introduces a new chapter.

The Book's Structure

This book is divided into eight chapters—the first chapter starts with a brief introduction to Docker and containerization. You will then take a 101 class in Docker—including installing, configuring, and understanding some jargon around Docker. In Chapter 3, you look at the book's project and learn how to configure the chatbot.

Chapters 4 to 6 dive into the meat of Docker, focusing on Dockerfile, Docker networks, and Docker volumes, along with practical exercises on how to incorporate each of these into your project. In Chapter 7, you learn about Docker Compose and see how you can run multi-container applications. Finally, you learn what container orchestrators are, get an overview of Kubernetes, and see how to set up Continuous Integration (CI) using GitHub Actions, with a Docker image built and pushed to the Docker Registry on each commit.

CHAPTER 1

Introduction to Containerization

This chapter looks at what Docker is, as well as what containerization is and how it is different from virtualization. Other subtopics covered include history of containerization, container runtimes, and container orchestration.

What Is Docker?

In order to answer this question, we need to clarify the word "Docker," because Docker has become synonymous with containers.

Docker Inc. is the company behind Docker. It was founded as dotCloud Inc. in 2010 by Solomon Hykes. dotCloud engineers built abstraction and tooling for Linux containers and used the Linux kernel features `cgroups` and namespaces with the intention of reducing complexity around using Linux containers. dotCloud made their tooling open source and changed the focus from their Platform As A Service (PaaS) business to containerization. Docker Inc. sold dotCloud to cloudControl, which eventually filed for bankruptcy.

Docker is the technology that provides for operating system level virtualization, known as *containers*. It is important to note that this is not the same as *hardware* virtualization. We will explore this later in the chapter. Docker uses the resource isolation features of the Linux kernel, such as `cgroups`, kernel namespaces, and OverlayFS, all within the same

© Sathyajith Bhat 2022
S. Bhat, *Practical Docker with Python*, https://doi.org/10.1007/978-1-4842-7815-4_1

physical or virtual machine. OverlayFS is a union-capable filesystem that combines several files and directories into one in order to run multiple applications that are isolated and contained from one other, all within the same physical or virtual machine.

Understanding Problems that Docker Solves

For the longest period, setting up a developer's workstation was a highly troublesome task for sysadmins. Even with complete automation of the installation of developer tools, when you have a mix of different operating systems, different versions of operating systems, and different versions of libraries and programming languages, setting up a workspace that is consistent and provides a uniform experience is nearly impossible. Docker solves much of this problem by reducing the moving parts. Instead of targeting operating systems and programming versions, the target is now the Docker engine and the runtime. The Docker engine provides a uniform abstraction from the underlying system, making it very easy for developers to test their code.

Things get even more complicated on the production landscape. Assume that you have a Python web application that is running on Python 2.7 on an Amazon Web Services EC2 instance. In an effort to modernize the codebase, the application had some major upgrades, including a change to Python version 3.5. Assume that this version of Python is not available in the packages offered by the Linux distribution currently running the existing codebases. To deploy this new application, you have the choice of either of the following:

- Replace the existing instance

- Set up the Python Interpreter by

  - Changing the Linux distribution version to one that includes the newer Python packages.

- Adding a third-party channel that offers a packaged version of the newer Python version.

- Doing an in-place upgrade, keeping the existing version of the Linux distribution.

- Compiling Python 3.5 from sources, which brings in additional dependencies.

- Or using something like `virtualenv`, which has its own set of tradeoffs.

Whichever way you look at it, a new version deployment for the application code brings about lots of uncertainty. As an operations engineer, limiting the changes to the configuration is critical. Factoring in an operating system change, a Python version change, and a change in application code results in a lot of uncertainty.

Docker solves this issue by dramatically reducing the surface area of the uncertainty. Your application is being modernized? No problem. Build a new container with the new application code and dependencies and ship it. The existing infrastructure remains the same. If the application doesn't behave as expected, then rolling back is as simple as redeploying the older container—it is not uncommon to have all the generated Docker images stored in a Docker Registry. Having an easy way to roll back without messing with the current infrastructure dramatically reduces the time required to respond to failures.

Containerization Through the Years

While containerization has exploded in popularity over the past couple of years, the concept of containerization actually goes back to the 1970s.

1979: chroot

The chroot system call was introduced in Version 7 of UNIX in 1979. The premise of chroot was that it changed the apparent root directory for the current running process and its children. A process initiated within a chroot cannot access files outside the assigned directory tree. This environment was known as the *chroot jail*.

2000: FreeBSD Jails

Expanding on the chroot concept, FreeBSD added support for a feature that allowed for partitioning of the FreeBSD system into several independent, isolated systems, called *jails*. Each jail is a virtual environment on the host system with its own set of files, processes, and user accounts. While chroot only restricted processes to a view of the filesystem, FreeBSD jails restricted activities of the jailed process to the whole system, including the IP addresses that were bound to it. This made FreeBSD jails the ideal way to test out new configurations of Internet-connected software, making it easy to experiment with different configurations while not allowing changes from the jail to affect the main system outside.

2005: OpenVZ

OpenVZ was quite popular in providing operating system virtualization for low-end *Virtual Private Server (VPS)* providers. OpenVZ allowed for a physical server to run multiple isolated operating system instances, known as *containers*. OpenVZ used a patched Linux kernel, sharing it with all the containers. Each container acted as a separate entity and had its own virtualized set of files, users, groups, process trees, and virtual network devices.

2006: cgroups

Originally known as *process containers*, `cgroups` (short for control groups) were started by Google engineers. `cgroups` is a Linux kernel feature that limits and isolates resource usage (such as CPU, memory, disk I/O, and network) to a collection of processes. `cgroups` have been redesigned multiple times, each redesign accounting for its growing number of use cases and required features.

2008: LXC

LXC provides operating-system level virtualization by combining Linux kernel's `cgroups` and support for isolated namespaces to provide an isolated environment for applications. Docker initially used LXC to provide the isolation features, but then switched to its own library.

Containers and Virtual Machines

Many people assume that since containers isolate the applications, they are the same as virtual machines. At first glance it looks like it, but the fundamental difference is that containers share the same kernel as the host.

Docker only isolates a single process (or a group of processes, depending on how the image is built) and all the containers run on the same host system. Since the isolation is applied at the kernel level, running containers does not impose a heavy overhead on the host as compared to virtual machines. When a container is spun up, the selected process or group of processes still runs on the same host, without the need to virtualize or emulate anything. Figure 1-1 shows the three apps running on three different containers on a single physical host.

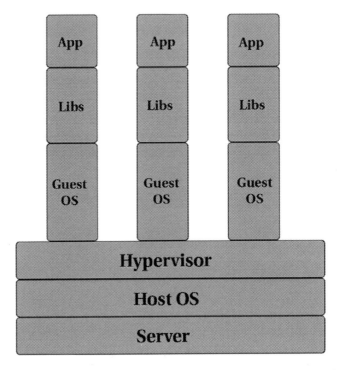

Figure 1-1. *Representation of three apps running on three different containers*

In contrast, when a virtual machine is spun up, the hypervisor virtualizes an entire system—from the CPU to RAM to storage. To support this virtualized system, an entire operating system needs to be installed. For all practical purposes, the virtualized system is an entire computer running in a computer. Now if you can imagine how much overhead it takes to run a single operating system, imagine how it'd be if you ran a nested operating system! Figure 1-2 shows a representation of the three apps running on three different virtual machines on a single physical host.

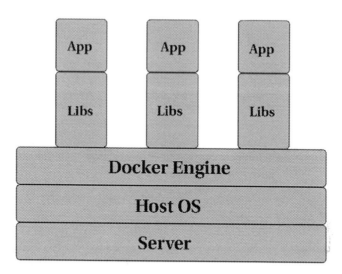

Figure 1-2. *Representation of three apps running on three different virtual machines*

Figures 1-1 and 1-2 give an indication of three different applications running on a single host. In the case of a VM, not only do you need the application's dependent libraries, you also need an operating system to run the application. In comparison, with containers, sharing the host OS's kernel with the application means that the overhead of an additional OS is removed. Not only does this greatly improve the performance, it also lets you improve the resource utilization and minimize wasted compute power.

Container Runtimes

A container image, when started and run, becomes a container. But for this to happen, there must be a piece of software to bootstrap the required resources to run a container. This software is called the *container runtime*. Docker implements a container runtime using the containerd project, which is now part of Cloud Native Computing Foundation's graduated project list.

`containerd` is not the only container runtime, however. There are other container runtime projects, such as `cri-o`, `rkt` (which is not in active development anymore), `runC`, and more.

OCI and CRI

With more container runtimes being developed, there was a need for a standard that would define what a container image is, the specifications of the runtime. That's where the Open Container Initiative (OCI) comes in.

OCI is an open governance structure for creating an industry-standard specification for container images and runtimes, free from vendor-specific features to promote an open ecosystem. The OCI currently has two specifications: the Runtime Specification and the Image Specification.

The Runtime Specification defines how a container runtime should unpack a container image into a filesystem and the steps to run the container. This ensures that the container will run accurately as expected, no matter which container runtime is in use.

The Image Specification defines an OCI Image format that contains the required definitions on how to create an OCI image. An OCI Image comprises the image manifest, a filesystem definition, and an image configuration. The image manifest contains the metadata about the contents and the dependencies of the image. An image configuration includes data such as application arguments and environment variables.

Container Runtime Interface (CRI) is a Kubernetes-specific term that defines how Kubernetes can interact with multiple container runtimes and bootstrap the containers. Before CRI, Kubernetes supported only the Docker runtime. With the requests coming in from the community to support more container runtimes, the Kubernetes team implemented a plugin interface for container runtimes. This plugin interface allows for Kubernetes to support interchangeable container runtimes, allowing for easy contributions from the community.

Docker and Kubernetes

With Kubernetes usage increasing in the industry, a question that comes up quite a lot is the difference between Docker and Kubernetes.

Kubernetes is an orchestrator for running containers and maintaining their lifecycle. Docker is multi-purpose software that can not only build container images but also run containers. While Docker can run and maintain lifecycles of containers not only on single nodes but also on multiple nodes using Docker Compose and Docker Swarm, Kubernetes has emerged as the de facto standard for container orchestration.

Docker and Kubernetes are complementary—Docker builds the container images while Kubernetes orchestrates the running of those containers. Kubernetes can also schedule running replicas of the containers over many nodes.

Chapter 8 takes a deeper look at container orchestration.

Summary

In this chapter, you learned a bit about Docker the company, Docker containers, and containers compared to virtual machines, as well as about the real-world problems that containers are trying to solve. You also took a brief look at what a container runtime is and how Docker and Kubernetes complement each other. In the upcoming chapter, you take an introductory tour of Docker and run a couple of hands-on sessions on building and running containers.

CHAPTER 2

Docker 101

Now that you understand a little bit better about how Docker works and why its popularity has exploded, in this chapter, you'll learn some different terminology associated with Docker. You will also learn how to Install Docker and understand Docker terms such as images, containers, Dockerfiles, and Docker Compose. You also work with some simple Docker commands on creating, running, and stopping Docker containers.

Installing Docker

Docker supports the Linux, macOS, and Windows platforms. It's straightforward to install Docker on most platforms and I'll get to that in a bit. Docker Inc. provides Community and Enterprise editions of the Docker platform.

The Enterprise edition has the same features as the Community edition, but it provides additional support and certified containers, plugins, and infrastructure. For the purposes of this book and for most general development and production uses, the Community edition is suitable, thus I will be using that in this book.

Installing Docker on Windows

Docker on Windows has some prerequisites that need to be met before you can install it. These include:

- Hyper-V support

- Hardware virtualization support: This is typically enabled from your system BIOS

- Only 64-bit editions of Windows 10 (Pro/Education/ Enterprise editions having the Anniversary Update v1607) are supported at the moment

If you look at these prerequisites, you'll notice that this looks like what a virtualization setup would require, yet you learned in the previous chapter that Docker is not virtualization. So why does Docker for Windows require features required for virtualization?

The short answer is that Docker relies on numerous features, such as namespaces and `cgroups`, and these are not available on Windows. To get around this limitation, Docker for Windows creates a lightweight Hyper-V container running a Linux kernel. If your computer has Windows 10 Home edition, you should install Docker Desktop with the WSL 2 backend. This is explained in the next section.

Let's focus on installing Docker CE for Windows. This section assumes that all the prerequisites have been met and Hyper-V is enabled. Head over to `https://store.docker.com/editions/community/docker-ce-desktop-windows` to download Docker CE.

Note   Make sure you select the Stable channel and click the Get Docker CE button.

You may be prompted to enable Hyper-V and Containers support as part of the install (see Figure 2-1).

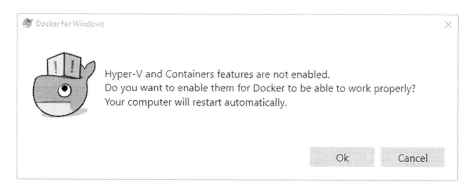

Figure 2-1. *Enable Hyper-V and containers feature*

Click OK and finish the installation. You may be required to restart your system, as enabling Hyper-V is a Windows system feature. Installing this feature requires a restart to enable it.

Once the install is complete, open a command prompt window (or PowerShell, if that is your preference) and type the following command to check that Docker is installed and is working correctly.

```
docker run --rm hello-world
```

If the install went fine, you should see the response shown in Listing 2-1.

Listing 2-1. Response from the docker run command on Windows

```
docker run --rm hello-world
Unable to find image 'hello-world:latest' locally
latest: Pulling from library/hello-world
b8dfde127a29: Pull complete
Digest: sha256:9f6ad537c5132bcce57f7a0a20e317228d382c3cd61edae1
        4650eec68b2b345c
Status: Downloaded newer image for hello-world:latest
```

13

```
Hello from Docker!
This message shows that your installation appears to be working
correctly.

To generate this message, Docker took the following steps:
 1. The Docker client contacted the Docker daemon.
 2. The Docker daemon pulled the "hello-world" image from the
    Docker Hub.
    (amd64)
 3. The Docker daemon created a new container from that image
    which runs the executable that produces the output you are
    currently reading.
 4. The Docker daemon streamed that output to the Docker
    client, which sent it to your terminal.

To try something more ambitious, you can run an Ubuntu
container with:
 $ docker run -it ubuntu bash

Share images, automate workflows, and more with a free Docker ID:
 https://hub.docker.com/

For more examples and ideas, visit:
 https://docs.docker.com/get-started/
 ...
```

We will take a deeper look later into what these commands mean,
so do not worry about understanding them. If you see the message
"installation appears to be working correctly," you should be good for now.

Installing Docker on Windows Using WSL2 Backend

About WSL

Announced with the 2016 Anniversary Update of Windows, Windows Subsystem for Linux (WSL) is a way for developers to run GNU/Linux applications from within Windows with no third-party Virtual Machine setup or having to dual boot into Linux. WSL supports most of the command-line applications and support for GUI applications is still in early preview mode.

With the first release of WSL, Microsoft bundled a custom compatibility layer for running Linux binary executables in Windows, without the need to rewrite or recompile the source code of the application. Microsoft did this using a translation layer, which intercepts Linux system calls from Linux applications and translates them into Windows systems calls.

For WSL2, Microsoft completely rearchitected how WSL works by shipping a lightweight Virtual Machine (VM) with a Linux kernel. This lightweight VM acts as the execution layer for Linux applications. Since the Linux applications are now natively run on the Linux kernel on the lightweight VM instead of using the translation layer, WSL2 supports all the features of the Linux kernel and improves the performance of Linux applications, as compared to the first edition of WSL.

While Virtual Machines bring up the problems of heavy resource usage, Windows manages the WSL2 Virtual Machine behind the scenes, complete with dynamic memory allocation, which increases/decreases the memory consumption as your application requests/releases it. WSL2 is still in early stages, and you might see some occasional problems/ slowdowns or heavy memory consumption. A quick reboot of Windows can mitigate these problems. You can also shut down and restart the VM, which will make Windows release the memory reserved by Windows.

Requirements for Installing and Enabling WSL2

Before you can install WSL2, ensure that your computer has Windows 10 64-bit version 1903 or higher. WSL2 will not work on versions lesser than 1903. You can check the version by typing winver on a Terminal prompt, as shown in Figure 2-2.

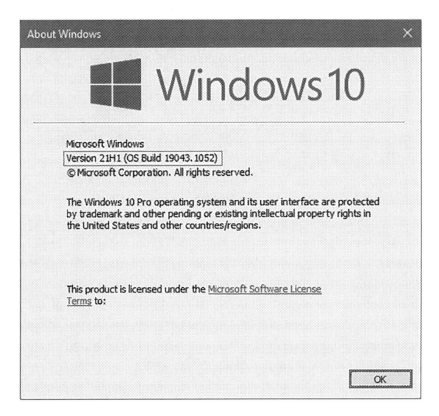

Figure 2-2. Check your Windows version, as highlighted in the red box

The installation steps for WSL2 are detailed on Microsoft's website at https://docs.microsoft.com/en-us/windows/wsl/install-win10. Follow the steps listed under Manual Installation Steps to install

WSL2. I highly recommend that you install Windows Terminal as well, as mentioned in the previous link, as it makes it easier to run Docker commands in WSL2.

Once you have WSL installed, run the following command to ensure WSL2 is set as the default version.

```
wsl --set-default-version 2
```

Install Docker Desktop with WSL2 Backend by downloading and running the installer at https://desktop.docker.com/win/stable/amd64/Docker%20Desktop%20Installer.exe. Once the install is complete, open a command prompt window (or PowerShell, if that is your preference) and type the following command to check that Docker is installed and is working correctly.

```
docker run -rm hello-world
```

If the install went fine, you should see the response in Listing 2-2.

Listing 2-2. Response from the docker run Command Using WSL

```
docker run --rm hello-world
Unable to find image 'hello-world:latest' locally
latest: Pulling from library/hello-world
b8dfde127a29: Pull complete
Digest: sha256:9f6ad537c5132bcce57f7a0a20e317228d382c3cd61edae1
        4650eec68b2b345c
Status: Downloaded newer image for hello-world:latest

Hello from Docker!
This message shows that your installation appears to be working
correctly.

[...]
```

The "Hello from Docker!" message indicates that Docker is installed and is working correctly. Note that the actual output is like the one in Listing 2-1 and has been trimmed in this instance.

Installing on macOS

Installing Docker for Mac is much like installing any other application. Go to https://store.docker.com/editions/community/docker-ce-desktop-mac, click the Get Docker for CE Mac (stable) link, and double-click the file to run the installer that is downloaded. Drag the Docker whale to the Applications folder to install it, as shown in the Figure 2-3.

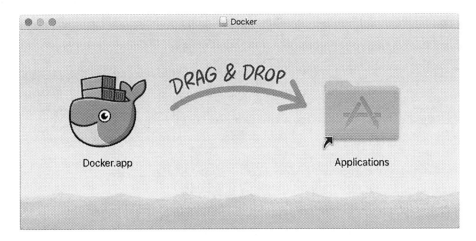

Figure 2-3. *Installing Docker for Mac*

Once Docker is installed, open the Terminal app and run this command to confirm the install was successful.

```
docker run --rm hello-world
```

If the install went fine, you should see the response shown in
Listing 2-3.

Listing 2-3. Response from the docker run Command on macOS

```
docker run --rm hello-world
Unable to find image 'hello-world:latest' locally
latest: Pulling from library/hello-world
b8dfde127a29: Pull complete
Digest: sha256:9f6ad537c5132bcce57f7a0a20e317228d382c3cd61edae1
        4650eec68b2b345c
Status: Downloaded newer image for hello-world:latest

Hello from Docker!
This message shows that your installation appears to be working
correctly.

[...]
```

The "Hello from Docker!" message indicates that Docker is installed
and is working correctly. Note that the actual output is like the one in
Listing 2-1 and has been trimmed in this instance.

Installing on Linux

To install Docker on Linux, visit `https://www.docker.com/community-`
`edition`. Select the distro you're using and follow the commands to install
Docker.

The following section outlines the steps needed to install Docker on Ubuntu.

1. Update the apt index:

    ```
    sudo apt-get update
    ```

2. Install the necessary packages required to use a repository over HTTPS:

    ```
    sudo apt-get install \
        apt-transport-https \
        ca-certificates \
        curl \
        software-properties-common
    ```

3. Install Docker's official GPG key:

    ```
    curl -fsSL https://download.docker.com/linux/ubuntu/gpg
    | sudo apt-key add -
    ```

4. Add Docker's stable repository:

    ```
    sudo add-apt-repository \
        "deb [arch=amd64] https://download.docker.com/linux/
        ubuntu \
        $(lsb_release -cs) \
        stable"
    ```

5. Update the apt package index:

    ```
    sudo apt-get update
    ```

6. Install Docker:

    ```
    sudo apt-get install docker-ce
    ```

Additional Steps

Docker communicates via a UNIX socket that is owned by the root user. You can avoid having to type sudo by following these steps:

Warning   The Docker group rights are still equivalent to the root user.

---

1. Create the Docker group:

    ```
    sudo groupadd docker
    ```

2. Add your user to the docker group:

    ```
    sudo usermod -aG docker $USER
    ```

3. Log out and log back in. Run the following command to confirm that Docker is installed correctly:

    ```
    docker run --rm hello-world
    ```

If the install went fine, you should see the response shown in Listing 2-4.

Listing 2-4. Response from the docker run Command on Linux

```
docker run --rm hello-world
Unable to find image 'hello-world:latest' locally
latest: Pulling from library/hello-world
b8dfde127a29: Pull complete
Digest: sha256:9f6ad537c5132bcce57f7a0a20e317228d382c3cd61edae1
        4650eec68b2b345c
Status: Downloaded newer image for hello-world:latest

Hello from Docker!
This message shows that your installation appears to be working
correctly.
[...]
```

The "Hello from Docker!" message indicates that Docker is installed and is working correctly. Note that the actual output is like the one in Listing 2-1 and has been trimmed in this instance.

Understanding Jargon Around Docker

Now that you have Docker installed and running, it's a good time to learn the different terms that are associated with Docker.

Layers

A *layer* is a modification applied to a Docker image as represented by an instruction in a Dockerfile. Typically, a layer is created when a base image is changed. For example, consider a Dockerfile that looks like this:

```
FROM ubuntu
Run mkdir /tmp/logs
RUN apt-get install vim
RUN apt-get install htop
```

In this case, Docker will consider the ubuntu image as the base image and add three layers:

- One layer for creating /tmp/logs

- One other layer that installs vim

- A third layer that installs htop

When Docker builds the image, each layer is stacked one upon the other and merged into a single layer using the union filesystem. Layers are uniquely identified using SHA-256 hashes. This makes it easy to reuse and cache them. When Docker scans a base image, it scans for the IDs of all the layers that constitute the image and begins to download the layers. If a layer exists in the local cache, it skips downloading the cached image.

Docker Image

Docker image is a read-only template that forms the foundation of your application. It is very much like a shell script that prepares a system with the desired state. In simpler terms, it's equivalent to a cooking recipe that has step-by-step instructions on creating the final dish.

A Docker image starts off with a base image—typically the one selected is of an operating system you are most familiar with, such as Ubuntu. On top of this image, you can add build your application stack, adding the packages as and when required. There are many prebuilt images for some of the most common application stacks, including Ruby on Rails, Django, PHP-FPM with `nginx`, and so on. On the advanced scale, to keep the image size as low as possible, you can also start off with slim packages such as Alpine or even scratch, which is Docker's reserved, minimal starting image for building other images.

Docker images are created using a series of commands known as *instructions* in a file known as the *Dockerfile*. The presence of a Dockerfile in the root of a project repository is a good indicator that the program is container-friendly. You can build own images from the associated Dockerfile and the built image is then published to a Registry. You will take a deeper look at Dockerfile in later chapters. For now, consider the Docker image as the final executable package that includes everything needed to run an application—the source code, the required libraries, and the dependencies.

Docker Tags

A *tag* is a name that uniquely identifies a specific version of a Docker Image. Tags are plain text labels, often used to identify specific details, such as the version, the base OS of the image, or the architecture of the Docker image.

Tagging a Docker image gives you the flexibility to refer uniquely to a specific version, making it easier to roll back to previous versions of a Docker image if the current image is not working as expected.

Docker Container

A Docker image, when run in a host computer, spawns a process with its own namespace and is known as a *Docker container*. The main difference between a Docker image and a container is the presence of a thin read-write layer known as the *container layer*. Any changes made to the filesystem of a container—such as writing new files or modifying existing files—are made to this writable container layer.

An important aspect to grasp is that when a container is running, the changes are applied to the container layer and, when the container is stopped/killed, the container layer is not saved. Hence, all changes are lost. This aspect of containers is not understood very well and for this reason, stateful applications and those requiring persistent data were initially not recommended to be adoptable as containerized applications. However, with Docker volumes, there are ways to get around this limitation. Chapter 5 covers Docker volumes in more detail.

Bind Mounts and Volumes

Recall that when a container is running, any changes to the container are present in the container layer of the filesystem. In the case of a container getting killed, the changes are lost, and the data is no longer accessible. Even when a container is running, getting data out of the container is not very straightforward. In addition, writing into the container's writable layer requires a storage driver to manage the filesystem. The storage driver provides an abstraction on the filesystem available to persist the changes and this abstraction often reduces performance.

For these reasons, Docker provides different ways to mount data into a container from the Docker host: volumes, bind mounts, or tmpfs volumes. While tmpfs volumes are stored in the host system's memory only, bind mounts and volumes are stored in the host filesystem.

Chapter 5 explores Docker volumes in detail.

Docker Repository

You learned earlier that you can leverage existing images of common application stacks—have you ever wondered where these are stored and how you can use them in building your application? A *Docker Repository* is a place where you can upload and store Docker images. These repositories allow for easy distribution of Docker images within your company or with the public.

Docker Registry

Docker Repositories need a central place to store the data—this central place is a *Docker Registry*. A Docker Registry is a collection of various Docker repositories. Docker Registries are hosted by third-party companies, or you can self-host them if you need to meet more strict compliance requirements. Docker Hub is a commonly used Docker Registry. Some other popular Docker Registries include:

- Google Container Registry

- Amazon Elastic Container Registry

- JFrog Artifactory

Most of these registries also allow for the visibility level of the images that you have pushed to be set as public/private. Private registries will prevent your Docker images from being accessible to the public, allowing you to set up access control so that only authorized users can use your Docker images.

Dockerfile

A *Dockerfile* is a set of instructions that tells Docker how to build an image. A typical Dockerfile includes the following:

- A FROM instruction that instructs Docker what the base image is

- An ENV instruction to pass an environment variable

- A RUN instruction to run some shell commands (for example, to install dependent programs that are not available in the base image)

- A CMD or an ENTRYPOINT instruction that tells Docker what executable is to be run when a container is started

As you can see, the Dockerfile instruction set has a clear and simple syntax, which makes it easy to understand. You will take a deeper look at Dockerfiles later in the book.

Docker Engine

Docker engine is a core part of Docker. Docker Engine is a client-server application that provides the platform, the runtime, and the tooling for building and managing Docker images, Docker containers, and many more. Docker Engine provides the following:

- Docker Daemon

- Docker CLI

- Docker API

Docker Daemon

The Docker daemon is a service that runs in the background of the host computer and handles the heavy lifting of most of the Docker commands. The daemon listens for API requests for creating and managing Docker objects such as containers, networks, and volumes. Docker daemon can also talk to other daemons for managing and monitoring Docker containers. Some examples of inter-daemon communication include communication Datadog for container metrics monitoring and Aqua for container security monitoring.

Docker CLI

Docker CLI is the primary way that you interact with Docker. Docker CLI exposes a set of commands that you can provide. The Docker CLI forwards the request to Docker daemon, which performs the necessary work.

While the Docker CLI includes a huge variety of commands and sub-commands, the most common commands that you will work with in this book are as mentioned:

```
docker build
docker pull
docker run
docker exec
```

Tip   Docker maintains an extensive reference of all the Docker commands on its Documentation page at `https://docs.docker.com/engine/reference/commandline/cli/`.

At any point in time, prepending help to a command will print the required documentation about the command. For example, if you're not quite sure on where to start with Docker CLI, you can type the following:

```
docker help
```

```
Usage:  docker COMMAND
```

```
A self-sufficient runtime for containers
```

```
Options:
        --config string        Location of client config files
                               (default
                               ".docker")
  -D, --debug                  Enable debug mode
  -H, --host list              Daemon socket(s) to connect to
  -l, --log-level string       Set the logging level
                               ("debug"|"info"|"warn"|"error"|"fatal")
                               (default "info")
[..]
```

If you want to know more about Docker pull, type the following:

```
docker help pull
```

```
Usage:  docker pull [OPTIONS] NAME[:TAG|@DIGEST]
```

```
Pull an image or a repository from a registry
```

```
Options:
  -a, --all-tags               Download all tagged images in
                               the repository
      --disable-content-trust  Skip image verification
                               (default true)
      --platform string        Set platform if server is
                               multi-platform
                               capable
```

Docker API

Docker also provides an API for interacting with the Docker engine. This is particularly useful if there's a need to create or manage containers from within applications. Almost every operation supported by the Docker CLI can be done via the API.

The simplest way to get started with the Docker API is to use `curl` to send an API request. Windows Docker hosts can hit the TCP endpoint:

```
curl http://localhost:2375/images/json
[{"Containers":-1,"Created":1511223798,"Id":"sha256:f2a91732
366c0332ccd7afd2a5c4ff2b9af81f549370f7a19acd460f87686bc7","
Labels":null,"ParentId":"","RepoDigests":["hello-world@sha2
56:66ef312bbac49c39a89aa9bcc3cb4f3c9e7de3788c944158df3ee017
6d32b751"],"RepoTags":["hello-world:latest"],"SharedSize":-
1,"Size":1848,"VirtualSize":1848}]
```

On Linux and Mac, the same can be achieved by using `curl` to send requests to the UNIX socket:

```
curl --unix-socket /var/run/docker.sock -X POST http://images/
json
[{"Containers":-1,"Created":1511223798,"Id":"sha256:f2a91732
366c0332ccd7afd2a5c4ff2b9af81f549370f7a19acd460f87686bc7","
Labels":null,"ParentId":"","RepoDigests":["hello-world@sha2
56:66ef312bbac49c39a89aa9bcc3cb4f3c9e7de3788c944158df3ee017
6d32b751"],"RepoTags":["hello-world:latest"],"SharedSize":-
1,"Size":1848,"VirtualSize":1848}]
```

Docker Compose

Docker Compose is a tool for defining and running multi-container applications. Much like how Docker allows you to build an image for your application and run it in your container, Compose uses the same images in combination with a definition file (known as the *compose file*) to build, launch, and run multi-container applications, including dependent and linked containers.

The most common use case for Docker Compose is to run applications and their dependent services (such as databases and caching providers) in a same simple, streamlined manner as running a single container application. Chapter 7 takes a deeper look at Docker Compose.

Docker Machine

Docker Machine is a tool for installing Docker engines on multiple virtual hosts and for managing the hosts. Docker Machine allows for creating Docker hosts on local as well as remote systems, including on cloud platforms such as Amazon Web Services, DigitalOcean, or Microsoft Azure.

Hands-on Docker

You can now try some of the things you've read in this chapter. Before you start exploring the various commands that are available, ensure that your Docker install is correct and that it is working as expected.

Tip   To makes things easy to read and understand, we used a tool called jq to process Docker's JSON output. You can download and install jq from `https://stedolan.github.io/jq/`.

Open a Terminal window and type the following command:

```
docker info
```

You should see a result like this one:

```
docker info
Containers: 0
 Running: 0
 Paused: 0
 Stopped: 0
Images: 1
Server Version: 17.12.0-ce
Storage Driver: overlay2
 Backing Filesystem: extfs
 Supports d_type: true
 Native Overlay Diff: true
Logging Driver: json-file
Cgroup Driver: cgroupfs
Plugins:
 Volume: local
 Network: bridge host ipvlan macvlan null overlay
 Log: awslogs fluentd gcplogs gelf journald json-file
      logentries splunk syslog
Swarm: inactive
Runtimes: runc
Default Runtime: runc
Init Binary: docker-init
containerd version: 89623f28b87a6004d4b785663257362d1658a729
runc version: b2567b37d7b75eb4cf325b77297b140ea686ce8f
init version: 949e6fa
Security Options:
 seccomp
  Profile: default
Kernel Version: 4.9.60-linuxkit-aufs
Operating System: Docker for Windows
```

```
OSType: linux
Architecture: x86_64
CPUs: 2
Total Memory: 1.934GiB
Name: linuxkit-00155d006303
ID: Y6MQ:YGY2:VSAR:WUPD:Z4DA:PJ6P:ZRWQ:C724:6RKP:YCCA:3NPJ:TRWO
Docker Root Dir: /var/lib/docker
Debug Mode (client): false
Debug Mode (server): true
 File Descriptors: 19
 Goroutines: 35
 System Time: 2018-02-11T15:56:36.2281139Z
 EventsListeners: 1
Registry: https://index.docker.io/v1/
Labels:
Experimental: true
Insecure Registries:
 127.0.0.0/8
Live Restore Enabled: false
```

If you do not see message something similar, refer to previous sections to install and validate your Docker install.

Working with Docker Images

Now you can try looking at your available Docker images. To do this, type the following command:

```
docker image ls
```

Here's a listing of the images available locally.

```
REPOSITORY       TAG        IMAGE ID        CREATED          SIZE
hello-world      latest     f2a91732366c    2 months ago     1.85kB
```

If you had pulled more images or run more containers, you'd have seen a bigger list. Let's look at the hello-world image. To do this, type the following:

```
docker image inspect hello-world
```

```
[
    {
        "Id": "sha256:f2a91732366c0332ccd7afd2a5c4ff2b9af81f549
            370f7a19acd460f87686bc7",
        "RepoTags": [
            "hello-world:latest"
        ],
        "RepoDigests": [
            "hello-world@sha256:66ef312bbac49c39a89aa9bcc3cb4f3
            c9e7de3788c944158df3ee0176d32b751"
        ],
        "Parent": "",
        "Comment": "",
        "Created": "2017-11-21T00:23:18.797567713Z",
        "Container": "fb0b4536aac3a96065e1bedb2b637a6019feec666
                c7699592206956c9d3adf5f",
        "ContainerConfig": {
            "Hostname": "fb0b4536aac3",
            "Domainname": "",
            "User": "",
            "AttachStdin": false,
            "AttachStdout": false,
```

```
    "AttachStderr": false,
    "Tty": false,
    "OpenStdin": false,
    "StdinOnce": false,
    "Env": [
        "PATH=/usr/local/sbin:/usr/local/bin:/usr/
        sbin:/usr/bin:/sbin:/bin"
    ],
    "Cmd": [
        "/bin/sh",
        "-c",
        "#(nop) ",
        "CMD [\"/hello\"]"
    ],
    "ArgsEscaped": true,
    "Image": "sha256:2243ee460b69c4c036bc0e42a48eaa59e8
            2fc7737f7c9bd2714f669ef1f8370f",
    "Volumes": null,
    "WorkingDir": "",
    "Entrypoint": null,
    "OnBuild": null,
    "Labels": {}
},
"DockerVersion": "17.06.2-ce",
"Author": "",
"Config": {
    "Hostname": "",
    "Domainname": "",
    "User": "",
    "AttachStdin": false,
    "AttachStdout": false,
```

```
        "AttachStderr": false,
        "Tty": false,
        "OpenStdin": false,
        "StdinOnce": false,
        "Env": [
            "PATH=/usr/local/sbin:/usr/local/bin:/usr/
            sbin:/usr/bin:/sbin:/bin"
        ],
        "Cmd": [
            "/hello"
        ],
        "ArgsEscaped": true,
        "Image": "sha256:2243ee460b69c4c036bc0e42a48eaa59e8
                2fc7737f7c9bd2714f669ef1f8370f",
        "Volumes": null,
        "WorkingDir": "",
        "Entrypoint": null,
        "OnBuild": null,
        "Labels": null
    },
    "Architecture": "amd64",
    "Os": "linux",
    "Size": 1848,
    "VirtualSize": 1848,
    "GraphDriver": {
        "Data": {
            "MergedDir": "/var/lib/docker/overlay2/5855bd20
                        ab2f521c39e1157f98f235b46d7c12c9d8
                        f69e252f0ee8b04ac73d33/merged",
```

```
            "UpperDir": "/var/lib/docker/overlay2/5855bd20a
                        b2f521c39e1157f98f235b46d7c12c9d8f6
                        9e252f0ee8b04ac73d33/diff",
            "WorkDir": "/var/lib/docker/overlay2/5855bd20ab
                        2f521c39e1157f98f235b46d7c12c9d8f69e
                        252f0ee8b04ac73d33/work"
        },
        "Name": "overlay2"
    },
    "RootFS": {
        "Type": "layers",
        "Layers": [
            "sha256:f999ae22f308fea973e5a25b57699b5daf6b0f1
            150ac2a5c2ea9d7fecee50fdf"
        ]
    },
    "Metadata": {
        "LastTagTime": "0001-01-01T00:00:00Z"
    }
    }
]
```

docker inspect provides a lot of information about the image. Of importance are the image properties Env, Cmd, and Layers, which tell you about the environment variables, the executable that runs when the container starts, and the layers associated with it.

The environment variables are as follows:

```
docker image inspect hello-world | jq .[].Config.Env
[
  "PATH=/usr/local/sbin:/usr/local/bin:/usr/sbin:/usr/bin:/
  sbin:/bin"
]
```

The startup command on the container is as follows:

```
docker image inspect hello-world | jq .[].Config.Cmd
[
  "/hello"
]
Layers associated with the image are as follows:
```

```
docker image inspect hello-world | jq .[].RootFS.Layers
[
  "sha256:f999ae22f308fea973e5a25b57699b5daf6b0f1150ac2a5c2ea9d
  7fecee50fdf"
]
```

Working with a Real-World Docker Image

Let's try looking at a more complex image. Nginx is a very popular reverse proxy server for HTTP/S (among others), as well as a load balancer and a webserver.

To pull down the nginx image, type the following:

```
docker pull nginx
```

```
Using default tag: latest
latest: Pulling from library/nginx
e7bb522d92ff: Pull complete
6edc05228666: Pull complete
cd866a17e81f: Pull complete
Digest: sha256:285b4
Status: Downloaded newer image for nginx:latest
```

Notice the first line:

```
Using default tag: latest
```

Since you did not provide a tag, Docker uses the default tag called latest. Docker Store lists the different tags associated with the image—so if you're looking for a specific tag/version, it'd be best to check on Docker Store. Figure 2-4 shows a typical tag listing of an image.

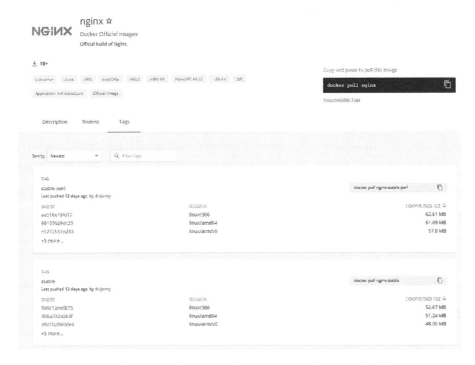

Figure 2-4. *Docker Store listing of nginx and the available tags*

Let's try to pull an image with a specific tag, called stable. The command remains the same as before. You must append the tag with a colon to explicitly mention the tag:

```
docker pull nginx:stable
stable: Pulling from library/nginx
b4d181a07f80: Already exists
e929f62bc938: Pull complete
ca8370516c99: Pull complete
```

```
6af693de7b22: Pull complete
c8fe6ce83489: Pull complete
7aa1fe8b4a84: Pull complete
Digest: sha256:a7c7c13
Status: Downloaded newer image for nginx:stable
docker.io/library/nginx:stable
```

The different hex numbers that you see are the associated layers of the image. By default, Docker pulls the image from Docker Hub. You can manually specify a different registry. This is useful if the Docker images are not available on Docker Hub and are stored elsewhere, such as an on-premises hosted artifactory. To specify a different registry, you have to prepend the registry path to the image name. So, if the registry is hosted on `docker-private-docker-registry.example.com`, the `pull` command will now be:

```
docker pull private-docker-registry.example.com/nginx
```

If the registry needs authentication, you can log in to it by typing `docker login` with the credentials, as shown here:

```
docker login -u <username> -p <password> private-docker-
registry.example.com
```

An unfortunate side-effect of this is that the entered password gets recorded and saved in plaintext in the shell history. Docker helpfully warns you about this message.

To prevent this, you can pipe in the password from a file into the standard input for Docker to read this using the following command, assuming that the password is stored in a file called `docker_password`

```
docker login -u <username> --password-stdin private-docker-
registry.example.com < docker_password
```

Windows users using PowerShell can use the Get-Content cmdlet to achieve the same as shown here:

```
Get-Content docker_password | docker login -u <username>
--password-stdin private-docker-registry.example.com
```

Now that you have the image, try starting a container. To start a container and run the associated image, type docker run.

```
docker run -p 80:80 nginx
```

Try making a curl request to see if the nginx webserver is running:

```
curl http://localhost:80
<!DOCTYPE html>
<html>
<head>
<title>Welcome to nginx!</title>
<style>
    body {
        width: 35em;
        margin: 0 auto;
        font-family: Tahoma, Verdana, Arial, sans-serif;
    }
</style>
</head>
<body>
<h1>Welcome to nginx!</h1>
<p>If you see this page, the nginx web server is successfully
installed and
working. Further configuration is required.</p>
```

```
<p>For online documentation and support please refer to
<a href="http://nginx.org/">nginx.org</a>.<br/>
Commercial support is available at
<a href="http://nginx.com/">nginx.com</a>.</p>

<p><em>Thank you for using nginx.</em></p>
</body>
</html>
```

This confirms that the `nginx` container is indeed up and running. In this, you see an extra flag, `-p`. This flag tells Docker to publish the exposed port from the Docker container to the host.

The first parameter after the flag is the port on the Docker host which must be published, and the second parameter refers to the port within the container. You can confirm that the image publishes the port using `docker inspect`:

```
docker image inspect nginx | jq .[].Config.ExposedPorts
{
  "80/tcp": {}
}
```

You can change the port on which the service is published on the Docker host by changing the first parameter after the `-p` flag, as follows:

```
docker run -p 8080:80 nginx
```

Now try doing a `curl` request to 8080 port:

```
curl http://localhost:8080
```

You should see the same response. To list all the running containers, type docker ps:

```
docker ps
```

```
docker ps
CONTAINER ID  IMAGE  COMMAND  CREATED  STATUS  PORTS  NAMES
fac5e92fdfac  nginx  "nginx -g 'daemon of..."  5 seconds ago
Up 3 seconds  0.0.0.0:80->80/tcp      elastic_hugle
3ed1222964de  nginx  "nginx -g 'daemon of..."  16 minutes ago
Up 16 minutes  0.0.0.0:8080->80/tcp   clever_thompson
```

The point to note is the names column. Docker auto-assigns a random name when a container is started. Since you should use more meaningful names, you can provide a name to the container by providing -n required-name as the parameter.

Tip   Docker names are of the format *adjective_surname* and are randomly generated, with the exception that if the adjective selected is boring and the surname is Wozniak, Docker retries the name generation.

Another point to note is that when you created a second container with port publishing to port 8080, the other container continues to run. To stop the container, you have to type this command:

```
docker stop <container-id>
```

where `container-id` is available from this list. If the stop was successful, Docker will echo the container ID back. If the container refuses to stop, you can issue a `kill` command to force stop and kill the container:

```
docker kill <container-id>
```

Let's try stopping a container. Type the following:

```
docker stop fac5e92fdfac
fac5e92fdfac
```

Now, let's try killing the other container:

```
docker kill 3ed1222964de
3ed1222964de
```

Let's confirm that the containers are no longer running, For this, type:

```
docker ps
```

CONTAINER ID	IMAGE	COMMAND	
CREATED	STATUS	PORTS	NAMES

So, what about the stopped containers—where are they? By default, `docker ps` only shows the active, running containers. To list all the containers, type:

```
docker ps -a
```

CONTAINER ID	IMAGE	COMMAND	CREATED
STATUS	PORTS	NAMES	
fac5e92fdfac	nginx	"nginx -g 'daemon of…"	
6 minutes ago	Exited (0) 4 minutes ago	elastic_hugle	
3ed1222964de	nginx	"nginx -g 'daemon of…"	
22 minutes ago	Exited (137) 3 minutes ago	clever_thompson	
febda50b0a80	nginx	"nginx -g 'daemon of…"	
28 minutes ago	Exited (137) 24 minutes ago		
objective_franklin			

```
dc0c33a79fb7           nginx           "nginx -g 'daemon of…"
33 minutes ago      Exited (137) 28 minutes ago
vigorous_mccarthy
179f16d37403           nginx           "nginx -g 'daemon of…"
34 minutes ago      Exited (137) 34 minutes ago       nginx-test
```

Even though the containers have been stopped and/or killed, these containers continue to exist in the local filesystem. You can remove the containers by typing:

```
docker rm <container-id>
docker rm fac5e92fdfac
fac5e92fdfac
```

Let's confirm that the container was indeed removed:

```
docker ps -a
CONTAINER ID           IMAGE           COMMAND                    CREATED
STATUS                 PORTS           NAMES
3ed1222964de           nginx           "nginx -g 'daemon of…"
28 minutes ago      Exited (137) 9 minutes ago  clever_thompson
febda50b0a80           nginx           "nginx -g 'daemon of…"
34 minutes ago      Exited (137) 30 minutes ago
objective_franklin
dc0c33a79fb7           nginx           "nginx -g 'daemon of…"
39 minutes ago      Exited (137) 34 minutes ago
vigorous_mccarthy
179f16d37403           nginx           "nginx -g 'daemon of…"
40 minutes ago      Exited (137) 40 minutes ago       nginx-test
```

You can see from this table that that container with the `fac5e92fdfac` ID is no longer shown and hence has been removed.

Similarly, you can list all the images present in the system by typing the following:

```
docker image ls
REPOSITORY              TAG        IMAGE ID       CREATED       SIZE
nginx                   1.12-alpine-perl          b6a456f1d7ae
4 weeks ago             57.7MB
nginx                   latest     3f8a4339aadd   6 weeks ago   108MB
hello-world             latest     f2a91732366c   2 months ago  1.85kB
kitematic/hello-world-nginx    latest            03b4557ad7b9
2 years ago             7.91MB
```

Let's try to remove the `nginx` image:

```
docker rmi 3f8a4339aadd
Error response from daemon: conflict: unable to delete
3f8a4339aadd (must be forced) - image is being used by stopped
container dc0c33a79fb7
```

In this case, Docker refuses to remove the image because there is a reference to this image from another container. Until you remove all the containers that use a particular image, you cannot remove the image altogether.

Summary

In this chapter you learned about how to install Docker on various operating systems. You also learned how to validate that Docker is installed and working correctly and some commonly used terms associated with Docker. Finally, you ran few practical exercises on Docker, including how to pull an image, run a container, list the running containers and, finally, how to stop and remove a container.

The next chapter takes a brief look at telegram, including how to create and register a bot with telegram, and how to run your Python-based Telegram Messaging bot, which will fetch posts from Reddit.

CHAPTER 3

Building the Python App

For many people getting into programming, one of their first issues is figuring out what they can build. Programming is seldom learned by just reading. Many people think they can read couple of guides and look at the syntax and then easily learn how to program. But programming takes hands-on practice.

For this reason, this book includes a sample Python project. The project is not very complicated at the start, but it's easy to continue working further on the project, extending and customizing it as you gain experience.

About the Project

Note   This book assumes you have basic knowledge of Python and have Python 3.6 or above installed.

To help you get acquainted with Docker, the book teaches you how to take an existing Python app, run it from the Python command line, introduce different Docker components, and then transition the app into a containerized image.

The Python app is a simple application with a bot interface using Telegram Messenger to fetch the last 10 stories from Reddit. Using Telegram, you can subscribe to a list of subreddits. The web application will check the subscribed subreddits for new posts and, if it finds new topics, it will publish the topics to the bot interface. That interface will deliver the message to Telegram Messenger, when requested by the user.

Initially, you will not be saving the preferences (i.e., the subreddit subscriptions) and will focus on getting the bot up and running. Once things are working fine, you will learn how to save the preferences to a text file and, eventually, to a database.

Setting Up Telegram Messenger

Before you can proceed, you need a Telegram Messenger account. To sign up, go to `https://telegram.org`, download the application for the platform of your choice, and install it. Once it's running, you will be asked to provide a cell phone number. Telegram uses this to validate your account. Enter your cell phone number, as shown in Figure 3-1.

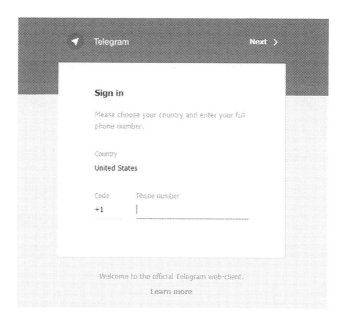

Figure 3-1. *Telegram signup page*

Once you enter your number, you should get a one-time password to log in. Enter the one-time password and sign in, as shown in Figure 3-2.

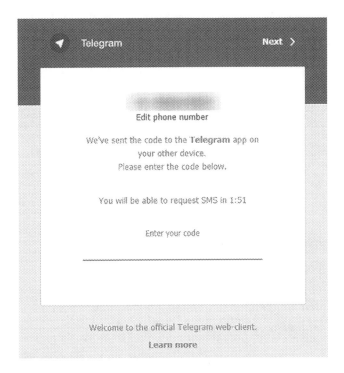

Figure 3-2. *Telegram's one-time password*

BotFather: Telegram's Bot Creation Interface

Telegram uses a bot called "BotFather" as its interface for creating new bots and updating them. To get started with BotFather, in the search panel type BotFather. From the chat window, type /start.

This will trigger BotFather to provide an introductory set of messages, as shown in Figure 3-3.

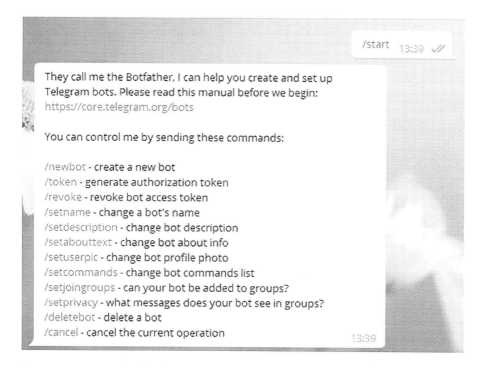

Figure 3-3. *BotFather's options*

Creating the Bot with BotFather

You will be using BotFather to generate a new bot. Start by typing /newbot in Telegram Messenger. This will trigger a series of questions that you need to answer (most of them are straightforward). Due to Telegram's restrictions, the username for a bot must always end with bot. This means that you might not get your desired username (see Figure 3-4).

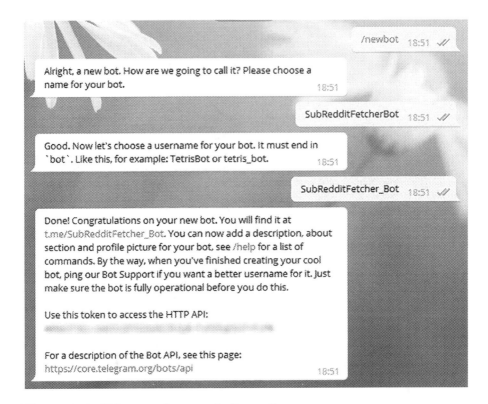

Figure 3-4. *Telegram bot ready for action*

Along with the link to the documentation, you will notice that Telegram has issued a token. HTTP is a stateless protocol—the webserver does not know and does not keep track of who is requesting the resource. The client needs to identify itself so that the webserver can identify the client, authorize it, and serve the request. Telegram uses the API token (henceforth, referred to as <token>, including in the code samples) as a way of identifying and authorizing bots.

Caution   The token is extremely sensitive. If it's leaked online, anyone can post messages as your bot. Do not check it in with your version control or publish it anywhere!

When working with APIs you are not familiar with, it's always good to use a good tool to test and explore the endpoints instead of typing the code right away. Some examples of REST API test tools include Insomnia, Postman, and curl.

Telegram's Bot API documentation is available at https://core. telegram.org/bots/api. To make a request, you have to include the <token>. The general URL is as follows:

```
https://api.telegram.org/bot<token>/METHOD_NAME
```

Let's try a sample API request that confirms the token is working as expected. Telegram Bot API provides a /getMe endpoint for testing the auth token. You can try it, first without the token, as shown in Listing 3-1.

Listing 3-1. Making a curl Request to Telegram API Without a Token

```
curl https://api.telegram.org/bot/getMe

{
  "ok": false,
  "error_code": 404,
  "description": "Not Found"
}
```

Without the bot token, Telegram doesn't honor the request. Now try the token, as shown in Listing 3-2.

Listing 3-2. Making a curl Request to Telegram API with a Valid Token

```
curl https://api.telegram.org/bot<token>/getMe

{
  "ok": true,
  "result": {
    "id": 495637361,
    "is_bot": true,
```

```
    "first_name": "SubRedditFetcherBot",
    "username": "SubRedditFetcher_Bot"
  }
}
```

You can see that, with the proper token, Telegram identifies and authorizes the bot. This confirms that the bot token is proper, and you can go ahead with the app.

Newsbot: The Python App

Newsbot is a Python script that interacts with the bot with the help of the Telegram Bot API. Newsbot does the following things:

- Continuously polls the Telegram API for new updates being posted to the bot.

- If the keyword for fetching new updates was detected, it fetches the news from the selected subreddits.

Behind the scenes, Newsbot handles these scenarios:

- If there's a new message starting with /start or /help, it shows simple help text about what to do.

- If there's a message starting with /sources followed by a list of subreddits, it accepts them as the subreddits from the applicable Reddit posts.

Newsbot depends on a couple of Python libraries;

- Praw or Python Reddit API Wrapper, for fetching posts from subreddits.

- Requests, one of the most popular Python libraries for providing a simpler, cleaner API for making HTTP requests.

Getting Started with Newsbot

To get started with Newsbot, download the source code of the bot. The source code is available on the GitHub repository of the book, at https://github.com/Apress/practical-docker-with-python.

If you're familiar with Git, you can clone the repo using the following command:

```
git clone https://github.com/Apress/practical-docker-with-python.git
```

As an alternative, you can click the green Code button and choose Download ZIP from the GitHub repository page to get the source code. Once you have cloned the repo or extracted the ZIP, change to the directory containing the source code by typing the following command:

```
cd practical-docker-with-python/source-code/chapter-3/python-app
```

Now install the dependencies. To do this, type the following:

```
pip3 install -r requirements.txt
```

---

pip (Pip Installs Packages) is a package manager that installs Python libraries. pip is included with Python 2.7.9 and later, and Python 3.4 and later. *pip3* indicates that you are installing libraries for Python 3. If pip is not installed, install it before proceeding.

The `-r` flag tells pip to install the required packages from `requirements.txt`.

---

pip will check, download, and install the dependencies. If all goes well, you should see the output in Listing 3-3.

Listing 3-3. The Output from a Successful pip Install

```
Collecting praw==3.6.0 (from -r requirements.txt (line 1))
  Downloading praw-3.6.0-py2.py3-none-any.whl (74kB)
Collecting requests==2.18.4 (from -r requirements.txt (line 2))
[...]
Installing collected packages: requests, update-checker,
decorator, six, praw
Successfully installed decorator-4.0.11 praw-3.6.0
requests-2.18.4 six-1.10.0 update-checker-0.16
```

If some packages were already installed, pip will not reinstall them and will inform you that the dependency is installed with a "Requirement already satisfied" message.

Running Newsbot

Let's start the bot. The bot requires an authentication token from Telegram that you created previously (referred to as <token>). This needs to be set to an environment variable named as NBT_ACCESS_TOKEN. Without this token, the bot will not run. To set this token, open a terminal and enter the following command, depending on your platform.

Windows users:

```
setx NBT_ACCESS_TOKEN <token>
```

Linux and macOS users:

```
export NBT_ACCESS_TOKEN=<token>
```

Now, start the Python script by typing the following command:

```
python newsbot.py
```

If all's well, you should be seeing periodic OK messages, as shown in Listing 3-4. This means that Newsbot is running and is actively listening for updates.

Listing 3-4. Output from Newsbot When It Is Running and Listening to Messages from Telegram

```
python newsbot.py
INFO: get_updates - received response: {'ok': True, 'result': []}
INFO: get_updates - received response: {'ok': True, 'result': []}
INFO: get_updates - received response: {'ok': True, 'result': []}
INFO: get_updates - received response: {'ok': True, 'result': []}
INFO: get_updates - received response: {'ok': True, 'result': []}
INFO: get_updates - received response: {'ok': True, 'result': []}
```

Sending Messages to Newsbot

In this section, you try to send a message to Newsbot to see if it accepts requests. From the BotFather window, click the link to the bot (alternatively, you can also search using the bot username). Click the Start button. This will trigger a /start command, which will be intercepted by the bot.

Notice that the log window shows the incoming request and the outgoing message being sent, as indicated in Listing 3-5.

Listing 3-5. The Newsbot Responding to Commands

```
INFO: get_updates - received response: {'ok': True, 'result': []}
INFO: get_updates - received response: {'ok': True, 'result': []}
INFO: get_updates - received response: {'ok': True, 'result': []}
INFO: get_updates - received response: {'ok': True, 'result':
[{'update_id': 720594461, 'message': {'message_id': 5, 'from':
{'id': 7342383, 'is_bot': False, 'first_name': 'Sathya', 'last_
```

name': 'Bhat', 'username': 'sathyabhat', 'language_code': 'en-
US'}, 'chat': {'id': 7342383, 'first_name': 'Sathya', 'last_
name': 'Bhat', 'username': 'sathyabhat', 'type': 'private'},
'date': 1516558659, 'text': '/start', 'entities': [{'offset': 0,
'length': 6, 'type': 'bot_command'}]}}]}
INFO: handle_incoming_messages - Chat text received: /start
INFO: post_message - posting
                    Hi! This is a News Bot which fetches news
from subreddits. Use "/source" to select a subreddit source.

Example "/source programming, games" fetches news from r/
programming, r/games.

Use "/fetch" for the bot to go ahead and fetch the news.
At the moment, bot will fetch total of 10 posts from all
subreddits
                    to 7342383
INFO: get_updates - received response: {'ok': True, 'result': []}

Figure 3-5 shows the Telegram Messenger window.

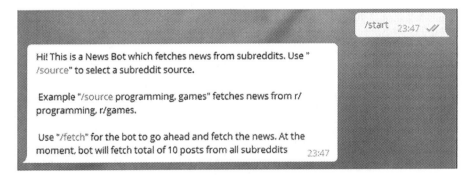

Figure 3-5. *The response from Newsbot to the start message*

Try setting a source subreddit. From the Telegram Messenger window, type the following:

```
/source python
```

You should get a positive acknowledgement from the bot, saying the source was selected (see Figure 3-6).

Figure 3-6. *Sources assigned*

Now you can tell the bot to fetch some news. To do this, type:

```
/fetch
```

The bot should send an acknowledgement message about fetching the posts. Then it will publish the posts from Reddit (see Figure 3-7).

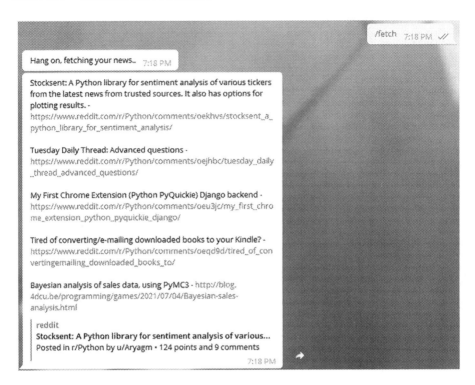

Figure 3-7. *Newsbot posting the top news from the Python subreddit*

The bot works; it's fetching the top posts as expected. In the next series of chapters, you learn how to move Newsbot to Docker.

Summary

In this chapter, you learned about the details of the book's Python Project, which is a chatbot. You also learned how to install and configure Telegram Messenger, how to use Telegram's BotFather to create the bot, how to install the dependencies for the bot and, finally, how to run the bot and ensure that it works correctly. In the next chapter, you dive deep into Docker, learn more about Dockerfiles, and containerize the Newsbot app by writing a Dockerfile for it.

CHAPTER 4

Understanding the Dockerfile

Now that you have a better understanding of Docker and its associated terminology, this chapter shows you how to convert your project into a containerized application using Docker. In this chapter, you learn what a Dockerfile is, including its syntax, and learn how to write a Dockerfile. With a better understanding of Dockerfiles, you can work toward the first step in writing a Dockerfile for the Newsbot app.

Dockerfile Primer

For a traditionally deployed application, building and packaging an application was often quite tedious. With the aim to automate the build and packaging of the application, people turned to different utilities, such as GNU Make, maven, Gradle, and so on, to build the application package. Similarly, in the Docker world, a Dockerfile is an automated way to build your Docker images.

The Dockerfile contains special instructions that tell the Docker Engine about the steps required to build an image. To invoke a build using Docker, you issue the `Docker build` command. Listing 4-1 shows a typical Dockerfile.

Listing 4-1. A Typical Dockerfile

```
FROM ubuntu:latest
LABEL author="sathyabhat"
LABEL description="An example Dockerfile"
RUN apt-get install python
COPY hello-world.py
CMD python hello-world.py
```

Looking at this Dockerfile, it's easy to see what we're telling the Docker Engine to build. However, don't let the simplicity fool you—Dockerfiles let you build complex conditions when generating your Docker images. When a Docker build command is issued, it builds the Docker images from the Dockerfile and a build context.

Build Context

A *build context* is a file or set of files available at a specific path or URL. To understand this better, say you have some supporting files that you need during a Docker image build—for instance, an application-specific config file that was generated earlier and needs to be part of the container.

The build context can be local or remote—you can even set the build context to the URL of a Git repository, which can come in handy if the source files are not located in the same host as the Docker daemon or if you want to test feature branches. You simply set the context to the branch. The build command would look like this:

```
docker build https://github.com/sathyabhat/sample-repo.
git#mybranch
```

Similarly, to build images based on your Git tags, the build command would look like this:

```
docker build https://github.com/sathyabhat/sample-repo.git#mytag
```

Working on a feature via a pull request? Want to try that pull request? Not a problem, you can even set the context to a pull request:

```
docker build https://github.com/sathyabhat/sample-repo.
git#pull/1337/head
```

The build command sets the context to the path or URL provided, uploading the files available to the Docker daemon and allowing it to build the image. You are not limited to a build context of an URL or path. If you pass an URL to a remote tarball (i.e., a .tar file), the tarball at the URL is downloaded onto the Docker daemon and the build command is issued with that as the build context.

Caution   If you provide the Dockerfile on the root (/) directory and set that as the context, doing so will transfer your hard disk contents to the Docker daemon.

Dockerignore

You should now understand that the build context transfers the contents of the current directory to the Docker daemon during the build. Consider the case where the context directory has a lot of files/directories that are not relevant to the build process. Uploading these files/directories can cause a significant increase in network traffic. A Dockerignore file, much like *gitignore*, allows you to define files that are exempt from being transferred during the build process.

The ignore list is provided by a file known as .dockerignore and when the Docker CLI finds this file, it modifies the context to exclude the files/patterns provided in the file. Anything starting with a hash (#)

is considered a comment and ignored. The following snippet shows a
sample .dockerignore file that excludes the temp, .git, and .DS_Store
directories:

```
*/temp*
.DS_Store
.git
```

BuildKit

With the 18.09 release of the Docker Engine, Docker overhauled their
container build system using BuildKit. BuildKit is now the default build
system for Docker. For most users, BuildKit works exactly as the legacy
build system. BuildKit has a new command output for Docker image
builds and, as a result, provides more detailed feedback about the build
process.

If you see output that's different from other learning resources, that
means they may have not been updated with the output from BuildKit.
BuildKit also tries to parallelize the build steps as much as possible, so you
can expect faster build speeds, especially for containers that have a lot of
Dockerfile instructions. For advanced users, BuildKit also introduces the
ability to pass secrets into the build stage without the secret being in the
final layer. The build output, when using BuildKit, is shown in Listing 4-2.
(Note that the sha output has been truncated due to space constraints.)

Listing 4-2. Build Output When BuildKit Is Enabled

```
docker build .
[+] Building 11.6s (6/6) FINISHED
 => [internal] load build definition from Dockerfile 0.1s
 => => transferring dockerfile: 84B    0.0s
 => [internal] load .dockerignore  0.1s
 => => transferring context: 2B 0.0s
```

```
=> [internal] load metadata for docker.io/library/
   ubuntu:latest 8.7s
=> [auth] library/ubuntu:pull token for registry-1.docker.io 0.0s
=> [1/1] FROM docker.io/library/ubuntu:latest@sha256:aba80b7 2.7s
=> => resolve docker.io/library/ubuntu:latest@sha256:aba80b7 0.0s
=> => sha256:aba80b7 1.20kB / 1.20kB 0.0s
=> => sha256:376209 529B / 529B  0.0s
=> => sha256:987317 1.46kB / 1.46kB 0.0s
=> => sha256:c549ccf8 28.55MB / 28.55MB  1.1s
=> => extracting sha256:c549ccf   1.2s
=> exporting to image 0.0s
=> => exporting layers  0.0s
=> => writing image sha256:f2afdc
```

As of writing this chapter, it is still possible to switch back to the legacy build process by setting the DOCKER_BUILDKIT flag, as shown in Listing 4-3.

Listing 4-3. Switching Back to the Legacy Build Process

```
DOCKER_BUILDKIT=0 docker build .

Sending build context to Docker daemon  2.048kB
Step 1/2 : FROM ubuntu:latest
latest: Pulling from library/ubuntu
c549ccf8d472: Already exists
Digest: sha256:aba80b77e27148d99c034a987e7da3a287ed455390352663
418c0f2ed40417fe
Status: Downloaded newer image for ubuntu:latest
 ---> 9873176a8ff5
Step 2/2 : CMD echo Hello World!
 ---> Running in d5ca2635eecd
Removing intermediate container d5ca2635eecd
 ---> 77711564634f
Successfully built 77711564634f
```

Unless you encounter any problems, I do not recommend switching back to the legacy build process. Stick to using Docker BuildKit. If you're not seeing the new build output, ensure that you have updated to the latest version of Docker.

Building Using Docker Build

You'll return to the sample Dockerfile a bit later. Let's start with a simple Dockerfile first. Copy the following snippet to a file and save it as Dockerfile:

```
FROM ubuntu:latest
CMD echo Hello World!
```

Now build this image using the docker build command. You'll see the response as shown in Listing 4-4. (Note that the sha output has been truncated.)

Listing 4-4. Response from Docker Engine as it Builds the Dockerfile

```
docker build .
[+] Building 11.6s (6/6) FINISHED
 => [internal] load build definition from Dockerfile0.1s
 => => transferring dockerfile: 84B  0.0s
 => [internal] load .dockerignore 0.1s
 => => transferring context: 2B0.0s
 => [internal] load metadata for docker.io/library/
    ubuntu:latest 8.7s
 => [auth] library/ubuntu:pull token for registry-1.docker.io 0.0s
 => [1/1] FROM docker.io/library/ubuntu:latest@sha256:aba80b7 2.7s
 => => resolve docker.io/library/ubuntu:latest@sha256:aba80b7 0.0s
```

```
=> => sha256:aba80b7 1.20kB / 1.20kB 0.0s
=> => sha256:376209 529B / 529B 0.0s
=> => sha256:987317 1.46kB / 1.46kB 0.0s
=> => sha256:c549ccf8 28.55MB / 28.55MB 1.1s
=> => extracting sha256:c549ccf  1.2s
=> exporting to image0.0s
=> => exporting layers  0.0s
=> => writing image sha256:f2afdc
```

You can see that the Docker build works in steps, each step corresponding to one instruction of the Dockerfile. Now try the build process again.

```
docker build .
[+] Building 0.1s (5/5) FINISHED
=> [internal] load build definition from Dockerfile 0.0s
=> => transferring dockerfile: 37B   0.0s
=> [internal] load .dockerignore  0.0s
=> => transferring context: 2B 0.0s
=> [internal] load metadata for docker.io/library/ubuntu:latest 0.0s
=> CACHED [1/1] FROM docker.io/library/ubuntu:latest   0.0s
=> exporting to image 0.0s
=> => exporting layers   0.0s
=> => writing image sha256:f2afdcc   0.0s
```

Note how much faster the build process is the second time around. Docker has already cached the layers and doesn't have to pull them again. To run this image, use the docker run command followed by the image ID f2afdcc:

```
docker run f2afdcc
Hello World!
```

So, the Docker runtime was able to start a container and run the command defined by the CMD instruction; hence, you get the output. Now, starting a container from an image by typing the image ID gets tedious fast. You can make this easier by tagging the image with an easy-to-remember name. You can do this by using the docker tag command, as shown here:

```
docker tag <image id> <tag name>
docker tag f2afdcc sathyabhat/hello-world
```

You'll look at deeper look at tags in the next section. Docker also validates that the Dockerfile has valid instructions and they are in the proper syntax. Consider the earlier Dockerfile, shown in Listing 4-5.

Listing 4-5. Dockerfile for Python with an Invalid Instruction

```
FROM ubuntu:latest
LABEL author="sathyabhat"
LABEL description="An example Dockerfile"
RUN apt-get install python
COPY hello-world.py
CMD python hello-world.py
```

If you try to build this Dockerfile, Docker will complain about an error, as shown here:

```
docker build -f Dockerfile.invalid .
[+] Building 0.1s (2/2) FINISHED
=> [internal] load build definition from Dockerfile.invalid  0.0s
=> => transferring dockerfile: 336B  0.0s
=> [internal] load .dockerignore  0.0s
=> => transferring context: 2B 0.0s
failed to solve with frontend dockerfile.v0: failed to create
LLB definition: dockerfile parse error line 6:
COPY requires at least two arguments, but only one was
provided. Destination could not be determined.
```

You'll get back to fixing this problem a little later in the chapter. For now, it's time to look at some of the commonly used Dockerfile instructions and at tagging images.

Tags

A *tag* is a name that uniquely identifies a specific version of a Docker image. Tags are plain-text labels often used to identify specific details, such as the version, the base OS of the image, or the architecture of the Docker image. Tagging a Docker image gives you the flexibility to refer uniquely to a specific version, which makes it easier to roll back to previous versions of a Docker image if the current image is not working as expected.

If a tag is not specified, Docker will apply a string called "latest" as the default tag. The "latest" tag is often the source of many problems, especially for new Docker users. Many believe that having "latest" as the tag would mean that the Docker image is the latest version of the image and would always be updated to the latest version. This is not true—latest was chosen as a convention but doesn't have any special meaning to it.

I do not recommend using latest as a tag, especially with production workloads. During development stages, omitting the tag will result in the "latest" tag being applied to every build. If there were a breaking change, since the tag is common, the previous images would get overwritten. This makes rolling back to the previous version of the image difficult unless you noted the SHA-hash of the image. Using specific tags makes it easier to determine, at a glance, what tag or version of Docker image is running on the container. Using specific tags also reduces the chance of breaking changes being propagated, especially if you tag your image as latest and have a breaking change or a bug. The next time your container crashes or restarts, it might pull the image with the breaking change or bug.

Docker images can be tagged and retagged using the docker tag command:

```
docker tag <image id> <tag name>
docker tag f2afdcc sathyabhat/hello-world
```

The tag names will typically have the Docker Registry prefixed to the tag name. If a registry name is not specified, Docker will assume the image is part of Docker Hub and will try to pull it from there. The tags can be assigned as part of the build process by passing the -t flag, as shown in Listing 4-6.

Listing 4-6. Adding a Tag When Building the Image

```
docker build -t sathyabhat/helloworld .

[+] Building 0.2s (5/5) FINISHED
=> [internal] load build definition from Dockerfile0.0s
=> => transferring dockerfile: 37B  0.0s
=> [internal] load .dockerignore 0.1s
=> => transferring context: 2B0.0s
=> [internal] load metadata for docker.io/library/
   ubuntu:latest0.0s
=> CACHED [1/1] FROM docker.io/library/ubuntu:latest  0.0s
=> exporting to image 0.0s
=> => exporting layers  0.0s
=> => writing image sha256:f2afdcc 0.0s
=> => naming to docker.io/sathyabhat/helloworld
```

Note that even though you did not mention docker.io as part of the tag, it was prefixed to the tag name, as mentioned. The last line tells you that the image was tagged successfully. You can verify this by searching for docker images:

```
docker images sathyabhat/helloworld
REPOSITORY               TAG      IMAGE ID      CREATED       SIZE
sathyabhat/helloworld    latest   f2afdccf8eeb  3 weeks ago   72.7MB
```

Dockerfile Instructions

When looking at a Dockerfile, you're mostly likely to run into the following instructions.

- FROM
- ADD
- COPY
- RUN
- CMD
- ENTRYPOINT
- ENV
- VOLUME
- LABEL
- EXPOSE

Let's see what they do.

FROM

As you learned earlier, every image needs to start from a base image. The FROM instruction tells the Docker Engine the base image to be used for subsequent instructions. Every valid Dockerfile must start with a FROM instruction. The syntax is as follows:

```
FROM <image> [AS <name>]
```

OR

```
FROM <image>[:<tag>] [AS <name>]
```

OR

```
FROM <image>[@<digest>] [AS <name>]
```

Where <image> is the name of a valid Docker image from any public/ private repository. As mentioned, if the tag is skipped, Docker will fetch the image tagged as latest.

WORKDIR

The WORKDIR instruction sets the current working directory for the RUN, CMD, ENTRYPOINT, COPY, and ADD instructions. WORKDIR is useful when you have multiple directories in the source code and you want some specific actions to be done within these specific directories. WORKDIR is also frequently used to set a separate location for the application to run in the container. The syntax is as follows:

```
WORKDIR /path/to/directory
```

WORKDIR can be set multiple times in a Dockerfile and, if a relative directory succeeds a previous WORKDIR instruction, it will be relative to the previously set working directory. Let's look at an example demonstrating this.

Consider this Dockerfile:

```
FROM ubuntu:latest
WORKDIR /app
CMD pwd
```

The Dockerfile fetches the latest tagged image from Ubuntu as the base image, sets the current working directory to /app, and runs the pwd command when the image is run. The pwd command prints the current working directory.

Let's try to build and run this and examine the output:

```
docker build -t sathybhat/workdir .
[+] Building 0.7s (6/6) FINISHED
 => [internal] load build definition from Dockerfile  0.0s
 => => transferring dockerfile: 36B 0.0s
 => [internal] load .dockerignore0.0s
 => => transferring context: 2B  0.0s
 => [internal] load metadata for docker.io/library/
    ubuntu:latest  0.6s
 => [1/2] FROM docker.io/library/ubuntu:latest@sha256:b3e2e4  0.0s
 => CACHED [2/2] WORKDIR /app 0.0s
 => exporting to image  0.0s
 => => exporting layers 0.0s
 => => writing image sha256:f8853df 0.0s
 => => naming to docker.io/sathybhat/workdir
```

Now you run the newly built image:

```
docker run sathybhat/workdir
/app
```

The result of pwd makes it clear that the current working directory is set as /app by way of the WORKDIR instruction. Modify the Dockerfile to add a couple of WORKDIR instructions, as shown here:

```
FROM ubuntu:latest
WORKDIR /usr
WORKDIR src
WORKDIR app
CMD pwd
```

Let's build and run the new image:

```
docker build -t sathybhat/workdir .
```

```
[+] Building 0.7s (8/8) FINISHED
 => [internal] load build definition from Dockerfile   0.0s
 => => transferring dockerfile: 121B   0.0s
 => [internal] load .dockerignore 0.0s
 => => transferring context: 2B 0.0s
 => [internal] load metadata for docker.io/library/
    ubuntu:latest   0.6s
 => [1/4] FROM docker.io/library/ubuntu:latest@sha256:b3e2e47   0.0s
 => CACHED [2/4] WORKDIR /usr 0.0s
 => CACHED [3/4] WORKDIR src   0.0s
 => CACHED [4/4] WORKDIR app   0.0s
 => exporting to image   0.0s
 => => exporting layers 0.0s
 => => writing image sha256:207b405   0.0s
 => => naming to docker.io/sathyabhat/workdir
```

Note that the image ID has changed, so that's a new image being built
with the same tag:

```
docker run sathybhat/workdir
/usr/src/app
```

As expected, the WORKDIR instructions of the relative directory have
appended to the initial absolute directory set. By default, the WORKDIR is
set as /, so any WORKDIR instructions featuring a relative directory will be
appended to /. Here's an example demonstrating this. Let's modify the
Dockerfile as follows:

```
FROM ubuntu:latest
WORKDIR var
WORKDIR log/nginx
CMD pwd
```

Build the image:

```
docker build -t sathyabhat/workdir .
```

```
[+] Building 1.8s (8/8) FINISHED
 => [internal] load build definition from Dockerfile    0.0s
 => => transferring dockerfile: 115B   0.0s
 => [internal] load .dockerignore   0.0s
 => => transferring context: 2B  0.0s
 => [internal] load metadata for docker.io/library/
    ubuntu:latest   1.6s
 => [auth] library/ubuntu:pull token for registry-1.docker.io  0.0s
 => CACHED [1/3] FROM docker.io/library/ubuntu:latest@
    sha256:b3e2e47 0.0s
 => [2/3] WORKDIR var    0.0s
 => [3/3] WORKDIR log/nginx    0.0s
 => exporting to image  0.0s
 => => exporting layers 0.0s
 => => writing image sha256:e7ded5d 0.0s
 => => naming to docker.io/sathyabhat/workdir
```

Now run it:

```
docker run sathyabhat/workdir
/var/log/nginx
```

Notice that you did not set any absolute working directory in the Dockerfile—the relative directories were appended to the default.

ADD and COPY

At first glance, the ADD and COPY instructions seem to be the same—they allow you to transfer files from the host to the container's filesystem. COPY supports basic copying of files to the container, whereas ADD has support for features like tarball auto extraction (i.e., Docker will automatically extract compressed files added from local directory) and remote URL support (i.e., Docker will download the resources from a remote URL).

The syntax for both are quite similar:

```
ADD <source> <destination>
COPY  <source> <destination>
```

The ADD instruction is useful when you're adding files from remote URLs or you have compressed files from the local filesystem that need to be automatically extracted into the container filesystem.

As an example, the following COPY instruction copies a single file called hugo to the /app directory in the container:

```
COPY hugo /app/
```

The following ADD instruction fetches a compressed file called hugo_0.88.0_Linux-64bit.tar.gz from the URL but doesn't automatically decompress the file:

```
ADD https://github.com/gohugoio/hugo/releases/download/v0.88.0/
hugo_0.88.0_Linux-64bit.tar.gz /app/
```

While the following ADD instruction will copy and automatically extract the contents of the compressed file to the /app directory in the container.

```
ADD hugo_0.88.0_Linux-64bit.tar.gz /app/
```

For Dockerfiles used to build Linux containers, both instructions let you change the owner/group of the files being added to the container. This is done using the --chown flag, as follows:

```
ADD --chown=<user>:<group> <source> <destination>
COPY --chown=<user>:<group> <source> <destination>
```

For example, if you want to add `requirements.txt` from the current working directory to the `/usr/share/app` directory, the instruction would be as follows:

```
ADD requirements.txt /usr/share/app
COPY  requirements.txt /usr/share/app
```

Both ADD and COPY support wildcards while specifying patterns. For example, having the following instructions in your Dockerfile will copy all the files with the .py extension to the `/apps/` directory of the image.

```
ADD *.py /apps/
```

```
COPY *.py /apps/
```

Note   Docker recommends using COPY over ADD, especially when it's a local file that's being copied.

There are some points to consider when choosing COPY versus ADD. In the case of the COPY instruction:

- If the `<destination>` does not exist in the image, it will be created.

- All new files/directories are created with UID and GID as 0—that is, as the root user. To change this, you can use the `--chown` flag.

- If the files/directories contain special characters, they need to be escaped.

- The `<destination>` can be absolute or relative paths. In case of relative paths, the relativeness will be inferred from the path set by the `WORKDIR` instruction.

- If the `<destination>` doesn't end with a trailing slash, it will be considered a file and the contents of the `<source>` will be written into `<destination>`.

- If the `<source>` is specified as a wildcard pattern, the `<destination>` must be a directory and must end with a trailing slash; otherwise, the build process will fail.

- The `<source>` must be within the build context. It cannot be a file/directory outside of the build context because the first step of a Docker build process involves sending the context directory to the Docker daemon.

In case of the `ADD` instruction:

- If the `<source>` is a URL and the `<destination>` is not a directory and doesn't end with a trailing slash, the file is downloaded from the URL and copied into `<destination>`.

- If the `<source>` is a URL and the `<destination>` is a directory and ends with a trailing slash, the filename is inferred from the URL and the file is downloaded and copied to `<destination>/<filename>`.

- If the `<source>` is a local tarball of a known compression format, the tarball is unpacked as a directory. Remote tarballs, however, are not uncompressed.

RUN

The RUN instruction will execute any command during the build step of the container. This creates a new layer that is available for the next steps in the Dockerfile. It is important to note that the command following the RUN instruction runs only when the image is being built. The RUN instruction has no relevance when a container has started and is running.

RUN has two forms, the shell form and the exec form. In the shell form, the command is written space-delimited, as shown here:

```
RUN <command>
```

This form makes it possible to use shell variables, subcommands, command pipes, and command chains in the RUN instruction itself.

Consider a scenario where you want to embed the kernel release version into the home directory of the Docker image. You can get the kernel release and version using the uname -rv command. This output can be then printed using echo and then redirected to a file called kernel-info in the home directory of the image. You can do this with the RUN instruction in shell form, as shown here:

```
RUN echo `uname -rv` > $HOME/kernel-info
```

In exec form, the command is written comma-delimited and surrounded by quotes, as shown here:

```
RUN ["executible", "parameter 1", " parameter 2"] (the exec form)
```

Unless you need to use shell features like chaining and redirection, it is recommended to use the exec form for the RUN instruction.

Due to the way layer caching works, it is always best to chain the package update and package install as a single RUN instruction. Consider a Dockerfile where the run instructions are as shown here:

```
RUN apt-get update
RUN apt-get install pkg1
RUN apt-get install pkg2
RUN apt-get install pkg3
```

When Docker builds this image, it caches the four layers created by the four RUN commands. To reduce the number of layers, and to prevent packages not being able to be installed due to the package cache being out of date, it is best to chain the update and installs, as shown here:

```
RUN apt-get update && apt-get install -y \
    pkg1 \
    pkg2 \
    pkg3 \
    pkg4
```

This creates a single layer with the packages to be installed, and any change in any of the packages will invalidate the cache and cause a new layer to be created with the updated packages. If you want to explicitly instruct Docker to avoid using the cache, then passing --no-cache flag to the docker build command will skip using the cache.

CMD and ENTRYPOINT

The CMD and ENTRYPOINT instructions define which command is executed when running a container. The syntax for both is shown here:

```
CMD ["executable","param1","param2"] (exec form)
CMD ["param1","param2"] (as default parameters to ENTRYPOINT)
CMD command param1 param2 (shell form)
ENTRYPOINT ["executable", "param1", "param2"] (exec form)
ENTRYPOINT command param1 param2 (shell form)
```

The ENTRYPOINT instruction is best when you want your container to function like an executable, and the CMD instruction provides the defaults for an executing container. Consider the Dockerfile shown here:

```
FROM ubuntu:latest
RUN apt-get update && \
    apt-get install -y curl && \
    rm -rf /var/lib/apt/lists/*
CMD ["curl"]
```

In this Docker image, Ubuntu is the base image, curl is installed on it, and curl is the parameter for the CMD instruction. This means that when the container is created and run, it will run curl without any parameters. Let's build the image for the Dockerfile shown here:

```
docker build -t sathyabhat/curl .
```

```
[+] Building 11.8s (6/6) FINISHED
 => [internal] load build definition from Dockerfile 0.0s
 => => transferring dockerfile: 50B  0.0s
 => [internal] load .dockerignore 0.0s
 => => transferring context: 2B  0.0s
 => [internal] load metadata for docker.io/library/
    ubuntu:latest  0.7s
 => CACHED [1/2] FROM docker.io/library/ubuntu:latest@
    sha256:b3e2e47  0.0s
 => [2/2] RUN apt-get update &&  apt-get install -y curl 10.7s
 => exporting to image  0.3s
```

```
=> => exporting layers  0.3s
=> => writing image sha256:8a9fc4b  0.0s
=> => naming to docker.io/sathyabhat/curl
```

You can see the result when you run the container:

```
docker run sathyabhat/curl
curl: try 'curl --help' or 'curl --manual' for more information
```

This is because curl expects a parameter to be passed. You can override the CMD instruction by passing arguments to the docker run command. As an example, try to curl wttr.in, which fetches the current weather.

```
docker run sathyabhat/curl wttr.in
docker: Error response from daemon: OCI runtime create failed:
container_linux.go:296: starting container process caused
"exec: \"wttr.in\": executable file not found in $PATH": unknown.
```

Uh oh, an error. As mentioned, the parameters after docker run are used to override the CMD instruction. However, you have passed only wttr. in as the argument, not the executable itself. For the override to work properly, you need to pass in the executable, which is curl, as well:

```
docker run sathyabhat/curl -s wttr.in
Weather report: Gurgaon, India

                    Haze
  _  -  _  -  _  -  24-25 °C
    _  -  _  -  _    ↘ 13 km/h
  _  -  _  -  _  -  3 km
                    0.0 mm
```

Passing an executable every time to override a parameter can be quite tedious. This is where the combination of ENTRYPOINT and CMD shines. You can set ENTRYPOINT to the executable while the parameter can be passed from the command line and will be overridden.

Modify the Dockerfile as follows:

```
FROM ubuntu:latest
RUN apt-get update && \
apt-get install -y curl
ENTRYPOINT ["curl", "-s"]
```

Build the image again:

```
docker build -t sathyabhat/curl .
```

```
[+] Building 0.7s (6/6) FINISHED
 => [internal] load build definition from Dockerfile.listing-
    4-x-5 0.0s
 => => transferring dockerfile: 157B 0.0s
 => [internal] load .dockerignore 0.0s
 => => transferring context: 2B    0.0s
 => [internal] load metadata for docker.io/library/ubuntu:latest    0.6s
 => [1/2] FROM docker.io/library/ubuntu:latest@sha256:b3e2e47    0.0s
 => CACHED [2/2] RUN apt-get update &&    apt-get install -y curl 0.0s
 => exporting to image    0.0s
 => => exporting layers  0.0s
 => => writing image sha256:7e31728  0.0s
 => => naming to docker.io/sathyabhat/curl
```

Now you can curl any URL by just passing the URL as a parameter, instead of having to add the executable as well.

```
docker run sathyabhat/curl wttr.in
Weather report: Gurgaon, India

                Haze
  _  -  _  -  _  -  24-25 °C
   _  -  _  -  _   \ 13 km/h
  _  -  _  -  _  -  3 km
                0.0 mm
```

Of course, curl is just an example here. You can replace curl with any other program that accepts parameters (such as load-testing utilities, benchmarking utilities, etc.) and the combination of CMD and ENTRYPOINT makes it easy to distribute the image.

Note that the ENTRYPOINT must be provided in exec form—writing it in shell form means that the parameters are not passed properly and will not work as expected. Table 4-1 is from *Docker's Reference Guide.* It explains the matrix of allowed ENTRYPOINT/CMD combinations, assuming p1_cmd, p1_entry and p2_cmd, p2_entry are the CMD and ENTRYPOINT variations of commands p1 and p2 that you want to run in the container.

Table 4-1. *Commands for ENTRYPOINT/CMD Combinations*

	No ENTRYPOINT	ENTRYPOINT exec_entry p1_entry	ENTRYPOINT ["exec_ entry", "p1_entry"]
No CMD	Error, not allowed	/bin/sh -c exec_entry p1_entry	exec_entry p1_entry
CMD ["exec_ cmd", "p1_ cmd"]	exec_cmd p1_ cmd	/bin/sh -c exec_entry p1_entry	exec_entry p1_entry exec_cmd p1_cmd
CMD ["p1_ cmd", "p2_ cmd"]	p1_cmd p2_cmd	/bin/sh -c exec_entry p1_entry	exec_entry p1_entry p1_cmd p2_cmd
CMD exec_ cmd p1_cmd	/bin/sh -c exec_cmd p1_ cmd	/bin/sh -c exec_entry p1_entry	exec_entry p1_entry / bin/sh -c exec_cmd p1_cmd

The following points are important to remember about the shell and exec forms:

- As mentioned earlier, you can specify RUN, CMD, and ENTRYPOINT in shell form and exec form. Which should be used will entirely depend on the requirements. But as general guide:

  - In shell form, the command is run in a shell with the command as a parameter. This form provides for a shell where shell variables, subcommands, commanding piping, and chaining are possible.

  - In exec form, the command does not invoke a command shell. This means that normal shell processing (such as $VARIABLE substitution, piping, etc.) will not work.

- A program started in shell form will run as a subcommand of /bin/sh -c. This means the executable will not be running as PID and will not receive UNIX signals. As a consequence, a Ctrl+C to send a SIGTERM will not be forwarded to the container and the application might not exit correctly.

ENV

The ENV instruction sets the environment variables to the image. The ENV instruction has two forms:

```
ENV <key> <value>
ENV <key>=<value> ...
```

In the first form, the entire string after the <key> is considered the value, including whitespace characters. Only one variable can be set per line in this form.

In the second form, multiple variables can be set at one time, with the equals (=) character assigning value to the key.

The environment variables set are persisted through the container runtime. They can be viewed using docker inspect.

Consider this Dockerfile:

```
FROM ubuntu:latest
ENV LOGS_DIR="/var/log"
ENV APPS_DIR /apps/
```

Build the Docker image:

```
docker build  -t sathyabhat/env .
[+] Building 1.7s (6/6) FINISHED
 => [internal] load build definition from Dockerfile.listing-
    4-x-6    0.0s
 => => transferring dockerfile: 50B 0.0s
 => [internal] load .dockerignore    0.0s
 => => transferring context: 2B   0.0s
 => [internal] load metadata for docker.io/library/
    ubuntu:latest   1.6s
 => [auth] library/ubuntu:pull token for registry-1.docker.io  0.0s
 => CACHED [1/1] FROM docker.io/library/ubuntu:latest@
    sha256:b3e2e47 0.0s
 => exporting to image   0.0s
 => => exporting layers 0.0s
 => => writing image sha256:23eb815 0.0s
 => => naming to docker.io/sathyabhat/env
```

You can inspect the environment variables by using the following command:

```
docker inspect sathyabhat/env | jq ".[0].Config.Env"
```

The output will be as follows:

```
[
 "PATH=/usr/local/sbin:/usr/local/bin:/usr/sbin:/usr/bin:/
 sbin:/bin",
  "LOGS_DIR=/var/log",
  "APPS_DIR=/apps/"
]
```

The environment variables defined for a container can be changed when running a container with the -e flag. In the previous example, change the LOGS_DIR value to /logs for a container. This is achieved by typing the following command:

```
docker run -it -e LOGS_DIR="/logs" sathyabhat/env
```

You can confirm the changed value by typing the following command at the terminal:

```
printenv | grep LOGS
LOGS_DIR=/logs
```

Type exit to close the interactive terminal of the container. To assign multiple environment variables, pass the additional environment variables using the -e flag, just as the first environment variable. In the previous example, if you were to override LOGS_DIR as well as APPS_DIR, it can be done using the following command:

```
docker run -it -e LOGS_DIR="/logs" -e APPS_DIR="/opt"
sathyabhat/env
```

```
printenv | grep DIR
LOGS_DIR=/logs
APPS_DIR=/opt
```

Type exit to close the interactive terminal of the container.

VOLUME

The VOLUME instruction tells Docker to create a mount point on the container and mount it externally from the host. For instance, an instruction like this:

```
VOLUME /var/logs/nginx
```

tells Docker to mark the /var/logs/nginx directory as a mount point, with the data being mounted from the Docker host. This, when combined with the volume flag on the Docker run command, will result in data being persisted on the Docker host as a volume. This volume can then be backed up, moved, or transferred using Docker CLI commands. You will learn more about volumes in a later chapter in this book.

EXPOSE

The EXPOSE instruction tells Docker that the container listens for the specified network ports at runtime. The syntax is as follows:

```
EXPOSE <port> [<port>/<protocol>...]
```

For example, if you want to expose port 80, the EXPOSE instruction is as follows:

```
EXPOSE 80
```

If you want to expose port 53 on TCP and UDP, the Dockerfile instruction is the following:

```
EXPOSE 53/tcp
EXPOSE 53/udp
```

You can also include the port number and whether the port listens on TCP/UDP or both. If not specified, Docker assumes the protocol to be TCP.

Note   An EXPOSE instruction doesn't publish the port. For the port to be published to the host, you need to use the -p flag with docker run to publish and map the ports.

Here's a sample Dockerfile that uses the nginx image with port 80 exposed in the container.

```
FROM nginx:alpine
EXPOSE 80
```

Build the container:

```
[+] Building 0.4s (5/5) FINISHED
 => [internal] load build definition from Dockerfile   0.0s
 => => transferring dockerfile: 50B 0.0s
 => [internal] load .dockerignore    0.0s
 => => transferring context: 2B   0.0s
 => [internal] load metadata for docker.io/library/
    nginx:alpine   0.2s
 => CACHED [1/1] FROM docker.io/library/nginx:alpine@
    sha256:9152859   0.0s
 => exporting to image  0.0s
 => => exporting layers 0.0s
 => => writing image sha256:33fcd52 0.0s
 => => naming to docker.io/sathyabhat/web
```

To run this container, you have to provide the host port to which it is to be mapped. Map it to port 8080 on the host to port 80 of the container. To do that, type the following command:

```
docker run -d -p 8080:80 sathyabhat:web
```

The -d flag makes the nginx container run in the background and the -p flag does the port mapping. Confirm that the container is running:

```
curl http://localhost:8080
<!DOCTYPE html>
<html>
<head>
<title>Welcome to nginx!</title>
<style>
    body {
        width: 35em;
        margin: 0 auto;
        font-family: Tahoma, Verdana, Arial, sans-serif;
    }
</style>
</head>
<body>
<h1>Welcome to nginx!</h1>
<p>If you see this page, the nginx web server is successfully
installed and
working. Further configuration is required.</p>

<p>For online documentation and support please refer to
<a href="http://nginx.org/">nginx.org</a>.<br/>
Commercial support is available at
<a href="http://nginx.com/">nginx.com</a>.</p>

<p><em>Thank you for using nginx.</em></p>
</body>
</html>
```

LABEL

The LABEL instruction adds metadata to an image as a key-value pair.

```
LABEL <key>=<value> <key>=<value> <key>=<value> …
```

An image can have multiple labels and is typically used to add some metadata to assist in searching and organizing images and other Docker objects. Docker recommends the following guidelines.

- For keys:
  - Authors of third-party tools should prefix each key with reverse DNS notation of a domain owned by them: for example, com.sathyasays.my-image.
  - com.docker.*, io.docker.*, and org.dockerproject.* are reserved by Docker for internal use.
  - Label keys should begin and end with lowercase letters and should contain only lowercase alphanumeric characters and the period (.) and hyphen (-) characters. Consecutive hyphens and periods are not allowed.
  - The period (.) separates the namespace fields.
- For values:
  - Label values can contain any data type that can be represented as a string, including JSON, XML, YAML, and CSV types.

Guidelines and Recommendations for Writing Dockerfiles

The following are some guidelines and best practices for writing Dockerfiles as recommended by Docker.

- **Containers should be ephemeral**. Docker recommends that images generated by Dockerfiles should be as ephemeral as possible. You should be able to stop, destroy, and restart the container at any point with minimal setup and configuration to the container. The container should ideally not write data to the container filesystem, and any persistent data should be written to Docker volumes or to data storage managed outside the container (for example, using a block storage like **Amazon S3**).

- **Keep the build context minimal**. You read about build context earlier in this chapter. It's important to keep the build context as minimal as possible to reduce the build times and the image size. This can be done by making effective use of the **.dockerignore** file.

- **Use multi-stage builds**. Multi-stage builds help in drastically reducing the size of the image without having to write complicated scripts to transfer/keep the required artifacts. Multi-stage builds are described in the next section.

- **Skip unwanted packages**. Having unwanted or nice-to-have packages increases the size of the image, introduces unwanted dependent packages, and increases the surface area for attacks.

- **Minimize the number of layers**. While not as big of a
  concern as they used to be, it's still important to reduce
  the number of layers in the image. As of Docker 1.10
  and above, only RUN, COPY, and ADD instructions create
  layers. With these in mind, having a minimal of these
  instructions or combining many lines of the respective
  instructions reduces the number of layers, ultimately
  reducing the size of the image.

Using Multi-Stage Builds

As of version 17.05 and above, Docker added support for multi-stage
builds, allowing complex image builds to be performed without the Docker
image being unnecessarily bloated. Multi-stage builds are especially useful
when you're building images of applications that require some additional
build-time dependencies but are not needed during runtime. Most
common examples are applications written using programming languages
such as Go or Javá, where prior to multi-stage builds, it was common to
have two different Dockerfiles. One was for the build and the other was for
the release and the orchestration of the artifacts from the build time image
to the runtime image.

With multi-stage builds, a single Dockerfile can be leveraged for build
and deploy images—the build images can contain the build tools required
for generating the binary or the artifact. In the second stage, the artifact
can be copied over to the runtime image, thereby considerably reducing
the size of the runtime image. For a typical multi-stage build, a build stage
has several layers—each layer for installing tools required to build the
application, generate the dependencies, and generate the application. In
the final layer, the application built from build stages is copied over to the
final layer and only that layer is considered for building the image. The
build layers are discarded, drastically reducing the size of the final image.

Although this book doesn't focus on multi-stage builds in detail, you will try an exercise on how to create a multi-stage build and see how much smaller using a slim image with multi-stage build makes the final image. More details about multi-stage builds are available on Docker's website at https://docs.docker.com/develop/develop-images/multistage-build/.

Exercises

BUILDING A SIMPLE HELLO WORLD DOCKER IMAGE

The start of the chapter introduced a simple Dockerfile that did not build due to syntax errors. In this exercise, you see how to fix that Dockerfile and add some of the instructions that you learned in this chapter.

Tip   The source code and associated Dockerfile are available on the GitHub repo of the book, at https://github.com/Apress/practical-docker-with-python, in the source-code/chapter-4/exercise-1 directory.

The original Dockerfile is as follows:

```
FROM ubuntu:latest
LABEL author="sathyabhat"
LABEL description="An example Dockerfile"
RUN apt-get install python
COPY hello-world.py
CMD python hello-world.py
```

Trying to build this will result in an error since hello-world.py is missing. Let's fix the build error. To do this, you need to add a hello-world.py that reads an environment variable, NAME, and prints Hello, $NAME!. If the environment variable is not defined, it will print "Hello, World!".

The contents of hello-world.py are as follows:

```
#!/usr/bin/env python3
from os import getenv

if getenv('NAME') is None:
        name = 'World'
else:
        name = getenv('NAME')
print(f"Hello, {name}!")
```

The corrected Dockerfile is as follows:

```
FROM python:3-alpine
LABEL description="Dockerfile for Python script which prints
Hello, Name"
COPY hello-world.py /app/
ENV NAME=Readers
CMD python3 /app/hello-world.py
```

Build the Dockerfile:

```
docker build -t sathyabhat/chap04-ex1 .
[+] Building 1.9s (8/8) FINISHED
 => [internal] load build definition from Dockerfile   0.0s
 => => transferring dockerfile: 37B 0.0s
 => [internal] load .dockerignore    0.0s
 => => transferring context: 2B   0.0s
 => [internal] load metadata for docker.io/library/python:3-
    alpine    1.7s
 => [auth] library/python:pull token for registry-1.docker.
    io  0.0s
 => [internal] load build context    0.0s
```

```
=> => transferring context: 36B 0.0s
=> [1/2] FROM docker.io/library/python:3-alpine@
   sha256:3998e97  0.0s
=> CACHED [2/2] COPY hello-world.py /app/    0.0s
=> exporting to image  0.0s
=> => exporting layers 0.0s
=> => writing image sha256:538be87 0.0s
=> => naming to docker.io/sathyabhat/chap04-ex1
```

Confirm the image name and size:

```
docker images sathyabhat/chap04-ex1
REPOSITORY               TAG      IMAGE ID       CREATED       SIZE
sathyabhat/chap04-ex1   latest   538be873d192   3 hours ago   45.1MB
```

Run the Docker image:

```
docker run sathyabhat/chap04-ex1
Hello, Readers!
```

Try overriding the environment variable at runtime. You can do this by providing the -e parameter with docker run:

```
docker run -e NAME=all sathyabhat/chap04-ex1
Hello, all!
```

Congrats! You've successfully written your first Dockerfile and built your first Docker image.

A LOOK AT SLIM DOCKER RELEASE IMAGE (USING MULTI-STAGE BUILDS)

In this exercise, you will build two Docker images. The first image uses a standard build with python:3 as the base image, whereas the second image gives an overview of how multi-stage builds can be utilized.

Tip   The source code and associated Dockerfile are available on the GitHub repo of the book at https://github.com/Apress/ practical-docker-with-python, in the source-code/ chapter-4/exercise-2/ directory.

Building the Docker Image Using a Standard Build

Create a requirements.txt file with the following content:

```
praw==3.6.0
```

Create a Dockerfile with the following content:

```
FROM python:3
COPY requirements.txt .
RUN pip install -r requirements.txt
```

Now build the Docker image:

```
[+] Building 7.2s (8/8) FINISHED
 => [internal] load build definition from Dockerfile    0.3s
 => => transferring dockerfile: 114B 0.0s
 => [internal] load .dockerignore 0.3s
 => => transferring context: 2B    0.0s
 => [internal] load metadata for docker.io/library/
    python:3  0.0s
 => [internal] load build context 0.6s
```

```
=> => transferring context: 54B  0.0s
=> [1/3] FROM docker.io/library/python:3   1.6s
=> [2/3] COPY requirements.txt . 0.2s
=> [3/3] RUN pip install -r requirements.txt 3.3s
=> exporting to image   1.6s
=> => exporting layers  1.5s
=> => writing image sha256:03191af  0.0s
=> => naming to docker.io/sathyabhat/base-build
```

The image was built successfully! Let's determine the size of the image:

```
docker images sathyabhat/base-build
```

Repository	Tag	Image ID	Created	Size
sathyabhat/base-build	latest	03191af	About a minute ago	895MB

The Docker image sits at a fairly hefty 895MB, even though you did not add any of your application code, just a dependency. Let's rewrite it to a multi-stage build.

Building the Docker Image Using a Multi-Stage Build

```
FROM python:3 as python-base
COPY requirements.txt .
RUN pip install -r requirements.txt

FROM python:3-alpine
COPY --from=python-base /root/.cache /root/.cache
COPY --from=python-base requirements.txt .
RUN pip install -r requirements.txt && rm -rf /root/.cache
```

The Dockerfile is different in that there are multiple FROM statements, signifying the different stages. In the first stage, you build the required packages using the python:3 image, which has the necessary build tools.

In the second stage, you copy the files installed in the first stage, reinstall them (notice this time that pip fetches the cached files and doesn't build them again), and then delete the cached install files. The build logs are shown here:

```
[+] Building 0.6s (13/13) FINISHED
 => [internal] load build definition from Dockerfile  0.2s
 => => transferring dockerfile: 35B 0.0s
 => [internal] load .dockerignore .1s
 => => transferring context: 2B  0.0s
 => [internal] load metadata for docker.io/library/python:3-
    alpine .2s
 => [internal] load metadata for docker.io/library/python:3 0.0s
 => [internal] load build context .1s
 => => transferring context: 37B 0.0s
 => [stage-1 1/4] FROM docker.io/library/python:3-alpine@
    sha256:3998e97 0.0s
 => [python-base 1/3] FROM docker.io/library/python:3 0.0s
 => CACHED [python-base 2/3] COPY requirements.txt .  0.0s
 => CACHED [python-base 3/3] RUN pip install -r requirements.
    txt  0.0s
 => CACHED [stage-1 2/4] COPY --from=python-base /root/.cache /
    root/.cache 0.0s
 => CACHED [stage-1 3/4] COPY --from=python-base requirements.
    txt .  0.0s
 => CACHED [stage-1 4/4] RUN pip install -r requirements.txt &&
    rm -rf /root/.cache 0.0s
 => exporting to image  0.1s
 => => exporting layers 0.0s
 => => writing image sha256:35c85a8 0.0s
 => => naming to docker.io/sathyabhat/multistage-build
```

Examining the size of the image using docker images shows you that using a multi-stage build has reduced the image size by quite a lot. This translates to reduced image sizes, faster application starts, and even reduced costs, as you are saving on bandwidth that is required to pull the container image.

```
docker images sathyabhat/multistage-build
```

Repository	Tag	Image ID	Created	Size
sathyabhat/ multistage-build	latest	35c85a8497b5	About a minute ago	54.2MB

WRITING A DOCKERFILE FOR NEWSBOT

In this exercise, you will write the Dockerfile for Newsbot, the Telegram chatbot project.

Tip   The source code and associated Dockerfile are available on the GitHub repo of the book at `https://github.com/Apress/practical-docker-with-python`, in the `source-code/chapter-4/exercise-3/` directory.

Let's review what you need for this project:

- A Docker image based on Python 3
- The project dependencies listed in `requirements.txt`
- An environment variable named NBT_ACCESS_TOKEN

Now that you have what you need, you can compose the Dockerfile. The general steps to composing a Dockerfile are as follows

1. Start with a proper base image.

2. Make a list of files required for the application.

3. Make a list of environment variables required for the application.

Layer Caching

When the image is built, Docker will cache the layers that it has pulled. This is evident from the build logs. Consider the following Dockerfile:

```
FROM ubuntu:latest
RUN apt-get update
```

The build log when you run docker build is shown here:

```
docker build -f Dockerfile .
[+] Building 8.1s (7/7) FINISHED
 => [internal] load build definition from Dockerfile  0.1s
 => => transferring dockerfile: 96B 0.0s
 => [internal] load .dockerignore   0.0s
 => => transferring context: 2B  0.0s
 => [internal] load metadata for docker.io/library/
    ubuntu:latest  1.8s
 => [auth] library/ubuntu:pull token for registry-1.docker.io  0.0s
 => CACHED [1/2] FROM docker.io/library/ubuntu:latest@
    sha256:b3e2e47 0.0s
 => [2/2] RUN apt-get update  6.0s
 => exporting to image  0.2s
 => => exporting layers 0.1s
 => => writing image sha256:a9824f6
```

The logs indicate that, instead of redownloading the layer for the base Ubuntu image, Docker uses the cached layer saved to disk. This applies to all the layers that are created—and Docker creates a new layer whenever it encounters RUN, COPY, or ADD instructions. Having the right order of instructions can greatly improve whether Docker will reuse the layers. This can not only improve the image build speed, but also reduce container start times by virtue of having lesser number of layers to download.

4. Copy the application files to the image using the COPY instruction.

5. Specify the environment variable with the ENV instruction.

Combining these steps, you arrive at this Dockerfile.

```
FROM python:3-alpine
WORKDIR /apps/subredditfetcher/
COPY . .
RUN ["pip", "install", "-r", "requirements.txt"]
CMD ["python", "newsbot.py"]
```

Now build the image:

```
[+] Building 0.9s (9/9) FINISHED
 => [internal] load build definition from Dockerfile    0.1s
 => => transferring dockerfile: 182B 0.0s
 => [internal] load .dockerignore 0.2s
 => => transferring context: 2B    0.0s
 => [internal] load metadata for docker.io/library/python:3-
    alpine 0.4s
 => [1/4] FROM docker.io/library/python:3-alpine@sha256:3998e97 0.0s
 => [internal] load build context 0.1s
 => => transferring context: 392B 0.0s
 => CACHED [2/4] WORKDIR /apps/subredditfetcher/ 0.0s
 => CACHED [3/4] COPY . .    0.0s
 => CACHED [4/4] RUN ["pip", "install", "-r", "requirements.
    txt"]  0.0s
 => exporting to image    0.1s
 => => exporting layers  0.0s
 => => writing image sha256:783b4c0  0.0s
 => => naming to docker.io/sathyabhat/newsbot
```

Now run the container. Take care to replace <token> with the Telegram Bot API key that you created in Chapter 3.

```
docker run -e NBT_ACCESS_TOKEN=<token> sathyabhat/newsbot
```

You should be seeing logs from the bot to ensure that it's running:

```
INFO: <module> - Starting up
INFO: get_updates - received response: {'ok': True, 'result': []}
INFO: get_updates - received response: {'ok': True, 'result': []}
INFO: get_updates - received response: {'ok': True, 'result': []}
```

If you see these logs, congratulations! Not only did you write the Dockerfile for Newsbot, but you also built it and ran it successfully.

Summary

In this chapter, you gained a better understanding of what a Dockerfile is by reviewing its syntax. You are now one step closer to mastering writing a Dockerfile for Newsbot.

CHAPTER 5

Understanding Docker Volumes

In the previous chapters, you learned about Docker and its associated terminologies and took a deeper look into how you can build Docker images using the Dockerfile. In this chapter, you look at data persistency strategies for Docker containers and learn why you need special strategies for data persistence.

Data Persistence

Traditionally, most compute solutions come with associated ways to persist and save data. In the case of virtual machines, a virtual disk is emulated, and the data saved to this virtual disk is saved as a file on the host computer. Cloud providers such as Amazon Web Services (AWS) provide different services, such as Amazon Elastic Block Store (EBS) and Amazon Elastic File Systems (EFS). These services provide an endpoint that can be mounted on the host virtual machine; data saved to these mount points is persisted and replicated.

When it comes to containers, the story is different. Containers were meant and designed for stateless workloads and the design of the container layers shows that. Chapter 2 explained that a Docker image is

© Sathyajith Bhat 2022
S. Bhat, *Practical Docker with Python*, https://doi.org/10.1007/978-1-4842-7815-4_5

a read-only template made of various layers. When the image is run as a container, a container with a small write-only layer of the data is created. This means that

- Data is tightly locked to the host and makes running applications that share data across multiple containers and applications difficult.

- Data doesn't persist when a container is terminated and extracting the data out of the container isn't possible in an easy manner.

- Writing to a container's write layer requires a storage driver to manage the filesystem. Storage drivers do not provide an acceptable level of performance in terms of read/write speeds and large amounts of data written to a container's write layer can lead to the container and the Docker daemon running out of memory.

Example of Data Loss Within a Docker Container

To demonstrate the features of the write layer, let's bring up a container from an Ubuntu base image. You will create a file within the Docker container, stop the container, and see the behavior of the container.

1. Start by creating a nginx container:

   ```
   docker run -d --name nginx-test  nginx
   ```

2. Open a terminal within the container:

   ```
   docker exec -it nginx-test bash
   ```

3.   Create a copy of nginx's default.conf to a new
     config file:

```
cd /etc/nginx/conf.d
cp default.conf nginx-test.conf
```

4.   You won't be modifying the contents of nginx-test.
     conf since it's immaterial. Now you need to stop the
     container. From the Docker host terminal, type the
     following:

```
docker stop nginx-test
```

5.   Start the container again:

```
docker start nginx-test
```

6.   Open a terminal within the container:

```
docker exec -it nginx-test bash
```

7.   Let's see if the changes are still around:

```
cd /etc/nginx/conf.d
ls
default.conf  nginx-test.conf
```

8.   Since the container was only stopped, the data
     persists. Let's stop it, remove the container, and then
     bring up a new one and observe what happens:

```
docker stop nginx-test
```

```
docker rm nginx-test
```

9.   Start a new container:

```
docker run -d --name nginx-test  nginx
```

10. Now that a new container is up and running,
     connect to the container's terminal:

```
docker exec -it nginx-test bash
```

11. Examine the contents of the conf.d directory of nginx:

```
cd /etc/nginx/conf.d
ls
default.conf
```

Since the container was removed, the write-only layer associated
with the container was also removed and the files created are no longer
accessible. For a containerized stateful application, such as an application
that requires a database, this means that when an existing container is
removed or a new container is added, the data from the previous container
is no longer accessible. To mitigate this, Docker offers various strategies to
persist the data.

- tmpfs mounts

- Bind mounts

- Volumes

tmpfs Mounts

As the name suggests, a tmpfs creates a mount in a tmpfs, which is a
temporary file storage facility. The directories mounted in tmpfs appear as
a mounted filesystem but are stored in memory, not to persistent storage
such as a disk drive.

tmpfs mounts are limited to Docker containers on Linux. A tmpfs
mount is temporary and the data is stored in Docker's hosts memory. Once
the container is stopped, the tmpfs mount is removed and the files written
to the tmpfs mount are lost.

To create a tmpfs mount, you can use the `--tmpfs` flag when running a container, as shown here:

```
docker run -it --name docker-tmpfs-test --tmpfs /tmpfs-mount
ubuntu bash
```

Let's examine the container:

```
docker inspect docker-tmpfs-test | jq ".[0].HostConfig.Tmpfs"
{
  "/tmpfs-mount": ""
}
```

This output tells you that there is a tmpfs config mapped to the /tmpfs-mount directory of the container.

tmpfs mounts are best for containers that generate data that doesn't need to be persisted and doesn't have to be written to the container's writable layer.

Bind Mounts

In bind mounts, the file/directory on the host machine is mounted into the container. In contrast, when using a Docker volume, a new directory is created within Docker's storage directory on the Docker host and the contents of the directory are managed by Docker.

Let's see how you can use bind mounts. You'll try to mount the Docker host's home directory to a directory called `host-home` within the container. To do this, type the following command:

```
docker run -it --name bind-mount-container -v $HOME:/host-home
ubuntu bash
```

Inspecting the created container reveals the different characteristics about the mount.

```
docker inspect bind-mount-container | jq ".[0].Mounts"

[
  {
    "Type": "bind",
    "Source": "/home/sathya",
    "Destination": "/host-home",
    "Mode": "",
    "RW": true,
    "Propagation": "rprivate"
  }
]
```

This output says that the mount is of bind type, the source (i.e., the directory of the Docker host being mounted) is /home/sathya (i.e., the home directory), and the destination of the mount is /host-home. The "Propagation" property refers to bind propagation—a property indicating whether the mounts created for a bind mount are reflected onto the replicas of that mount. Bind propagation is applicable only to Linux hosts. For bind mounts, this property typically doesn't need to be modified. The RW flag indicates that the mounted directory can be written to. Let's examine the contents of the host-home to see that the mounts are indeed proper.

1. Open the container's interactive terminal using the following command:

   ```
   docker run -it -v $HOME:/host-home ubuntu bash
   ```

2. In the terminal of the container, type the following:

   ```
   cd /host-home
   ls
   ```

3. The output of the command should be a listing of
    your Docker hosts' home directory. Try creating a
    file in the host-home directory. For this, type the
    following command:

```
cd /host-home
echo "This is a file created from container having
kernel `uname -r`" > host-home-file.txt
```

This command creates a file called host-home-file.txt, which
contains the text "This is a file created from container having
kernel 4.9.87-linuxkit-aufs" in the /host-home directory of the
container. Note the content will vary based on the host OS and kernel
version.

Since this is a bind mount of the home directory of the Docker host, the
file should also be created in the home directory of the Docker host. You
can see if this is indeed the case.

1. Open a new terminal window in your Docker host
    and type the following command:

```
cd ~
ls host-home-file.txt
```

2. You should be seeing this output, indicating the
    presence of the file:

```
ls host-home-file.txt
host-home-file.txt
```

3. Now check the contexts of the file:

```
cat host-home-file.txt
```

This file should have the same contents as you saw in the previous section. This confirms that the file created in the container is indeed available outside the container. Since you are concerned with data persistence after the container has been stopped, removed, and started again, let's see what happens.

Stop the container by entering the following command in the Docker host terminal.

```
docker stop bind-mount-container
docker rm bind-mount-container
```

Confirm that the file on the Docker host is still present:

```
cat ~/host-home-file.txt
This is a file created from container having kernel
4.9.87-linuxkit-aufs
```

Bind mounts are of immense help and are most often used during the development phase of an application. By having bind mounts, you can prepare the application for production by using the same container as production while mounting the source directory as a bind mount. This allows developers to have rapid code-test-iterate cycles without requiring the need to rebuild the Docker image.

Caution   Remember with bind mounts, the data flow goes both ways on the Docker host as well as on the container. Any destructive actions (such as deleting a directory) will negatively impact the Docker host as well.

As the caution, take utmost care when mounting the host OS directory into the container as a bind mount. This is even more important if the mounted directory is a broad one—such as the home directory (as shown previously) or the root directory. A script gone rogue or a mistaken `rm -rf` command can completely bring down the Docker host. To mitigate this, you can create a bind mount with a read-only option so that the directory is mounted read-only.

To do this, you can provide a read-only parameter with the docker run command. The commands are as follows:

```
docker run -it --name read-only-bind-mount -v $HOME:/host-
home:ro ubuntu bash
```

Now inspect the container that was created:

```
docker inspect read-only-bind-mount | jq ".[0].Mounts"
[
  {
    "Type": "bind",
    "Source": "/home/sathya",
    "Destination": "/host-home",
    "Mode": "ro",
    "RW": false,
    "Propagation": "rprivate"
  }
]
```

You can see that the "RW" flag is now false and the Mode is set to read-only (ro). Let's try writing to the file as earlier.

Open the container terminal:

```
docker run -it --name read-only-bind-mount -v $HOME:/host-
home:ro ubuntu bash
```

Typo the following command to create a file in the container:

```
echo "This is a file created from container having kernel
`uname -r`" > host-home-file.txt
bash: host-home-file.txt: Read-only file system
```

The write fails and bash tells you that it was because the filesystem is mounted read-only. Any destructive operations are also met with the same error:

```
rm host-home-file.txt
rm: cannot remove 'host-home-file.txt': Read-only file system
```

Docker Volumes

Docker volulmes are the current recommended method of persisting data stored in containers. Volumes are completely managed by Docker and have many advantages over bind mounts:

- Volumes are easier to back up or transfer than bind mounts.

- Volumes work on both Linux and Windows containers.

- Volumes can be shared among multiple containers without problems.

Docker Volume Subcommands

Docker exposes the Volume API as a series of subcommands. The commands are as follows:

- `docker volume create`

- `docker volume inspect`

- `docker volume ls`

- `docker volume prune`

- `docker volume rm`

Volume Create

The volume create subcommand is used to create named volumes. The most common use case is to generate a named volume. The usage for the command is as follows:

```
docker volume create --name=<name of the volume> --label=<any
extra metadata>
```

Tip   Docker object labels are discussed in Chapter 4.

For example, this command Creates a named volume called nginx-volume:

```
docker volume create --name=nginx-volume
```

Volume Inspect

The volume inspect command displays detailed information about a volume. The usage for this command is as follows:

```
docker volume inspect <volume-name>
```

Taking the example of the nginx-volume name, you can find more details by typing:

```
docker volume inspect nginx-volume
```

This will bring up the following result:

```
docker volume inspect nginx-volume
[
    {
        "CreatedAt": "2018-04-17T13:51:02Z",
        "Driver": "local",
```

```
        "Labels": {},
        "Mountpoint": "/var/lib/docker/volumes/nginx-volume/
        _data",
        "Name": "nginx-volume",
        "Options": {},
        "Scope": "local"
    }
]
```

This command is useful when you want to copy/move/take a backup of a volume. The mount path property lists the location on the Docker host, which is where the file containing the data of the volume is saved.

List Volumes

The volume ls command shows all the volumes present in the host. The usage is as follows:

```
docker volume ls
```

Prune Volumes

The volume prune command removes all unused local volumes. The usage is as follows:

```
docker volume prune
```

Docker considers volumes that are not used by at least one container unused. Since unused volumes can end up using a considerable amount of disk space, it's not a bad idea to run the prune command at regular intervals, especially on local development machines. You can append --force to the end of command, which will not ask for confirmation of deletion when the command is run.

Remove Volumes

The `volume rm` command removes volumes whose names are provided as parameters. The usage is as follows:

```
docker volume rm <name>
```

In the case of the volume created previously, the command would be as follows:

```
docker volume rm nginx-volume
```

Docker will not remove a volume that is in use and will return an error. For instance, if you try to delete the `nginx-volume` volume, which is attached to the container, you will get the following error message:

```
docker volume rm nginx-volume
```

```
Error response from daemon: unable to remove volume: remove
nginx-volume: volume is in use - [6074757a]
```

Note   Even if the container is stopped, Docker will consider the volume to be in use.

The long piece of identifier is the ID of the container associated with the volume. If the volume is associated with multiple containers, all the container IDs will be listed. More details about the associated container can be found by using the `docker inspect` command, as follows:

```
docker inspect 6074757a
```

Using Volumes When Starting a Container

The command for creating a container with a volume attached is shown here:

```
docker run --name container-with-volume -v data:/data ubuntu
```

In this example, a container called container-with-volume is created with a volume called data being mapped to the /data directory inside the container. When using volumes, instead of providing the full path of the host directory, you provide a volume name where the data will be stored. Behind the scenes, Docker will create and manage this volume by mapping it to a directory on the host.

Let's examine the container that was created using the following command:

```
docker inspect container-with-volume | jq ".[0].Mounts"
[
  {
    "Type": "volume",
    "Name": "data",
    "Source": "/var/lib/docker/volumes/data/_data",
    "Destination": "/data",
    "Driver": "local",
    "Mode": "z",
    "RW": true,
    "Propagation": ""
  }
]
```

Looking at the mounts section, you can conclude that Docker created a new volume called data with the contents of the volume being managed by Docker in the host directory of /var/lib/docker/volumes/data/_data. This volume is mounted to the /data directory of the container.

These volumes can also be generated ahead of time using the following command:

```
docker volume create info
```

You can use `docker volume inspect` to examine the volume's properties:

```
docker volume inspect info
[
    {
        "CreatedAt": "2021-07-27T19:23:00Z",
        "Driver": "local",
        "Labels": {},
        "Mountpoint": "/var/lib/docker/volumes/info/_data",
        "Name": "images",
        "Options": {},
        "Scope": "local"
    }
]
```

You can now refer to this volume when creating/running a container, as shown here:

```
docker run -it --name info-container -v info:/container-info
ubuntu bash
```

Let's try to create the same file as earlier. From the terminal within the container, type the following:

```
echo "This is a file created from container having kernel
`uname -r`" > /container-info/docker_kernel_info.txt
```

Exit the container, and then stop and remove the container using the following commands:

```
exit
docker stop info-container
docker rm info-container
```

In the absence of volumes, when the container was removed, its writable layer would be removed as well. Let's see what happens when you launch a new container with the volume attached. Remember that this is not a bind mount, so you are not explicitly forwarding any of the directories from the Docker host. The following command will start a shell on the container named new-info-container with a volume called info mounted into the /container-info directory in the container.

```
docker run -it --name new-info-container -v info:/container-
info ubuntu bash
```

Examine the contents of the /data-volume directory of the container, as follows:

```
cd /container-info/
ls
docker-kernel-info.txt
```

Examine the contents of docker-kernel-info.txt, as follows:

```
cat docker_kernel_info.txt
This is a file created from container having kernel
4.9.87-linuxkit-aufs.
```

When you write a file into a directory that is mounted and mapped to a volume, the data is persisted in the volume. When you launch a new container, providing the volume name along with the run command attaches the volume to the container, making any previously saved data available to the newly launched container.

The VOLUME Instruction in Dockerfiles

The VOLUME instruction marks the path mentioned after the instruction as an externally stored data volume that's managed by Docker. The syntax is as shown:

```
VOLUME ["/data-volume"]
```

The paths mentioned after the instruction can be a JSON array or an array of paths separated by space.

Note   The VOLUME instruction in a Dockerfile doesn't support named volumes. As a result, when the container runs, the volume name will be an autogenerated name.

Exercises

┌──┐
│ **BUILDING AND RUNNING AN NGINX CONTAINER WITH VOLUMES AND**   │
│ **BIND MOUNTS**   │
└──┘

In this exercise, you will build an nginx Docker image with a Docker volume attached that contains a custom nginx configuration. In the second part of the exercise, you will attach a bind mount and a volume containing a static web page and a custom nginx configuration. The intent of the exercise is to help you understand how to leverage volumes and bind mounts to make local development easy.

Tip   The source code and associated Dockerfile are available on the GitHub repo of this book at https://github.com/Apress/practical-docker-with-python, in the source-code/chapter-5/exercise-1 directory.

Start with the Dockerfile, as follows.

```
FROM nginx:alpine
COPY default.conf /etc/nginx/conf.d
VOLUME ["/var/lib"]
EXPOSE 80
```

This Dockerfile takes a base nginx image, overwrites the default.
conf nginx configuration file with the custom default.conf nginx
configuration file, and declares /var/lib as a volume. You can build this by
using the following command in the docker-volume-bind-mount directory
present in the repo:

```
docker build -t sathyabhat/nginx-volume .
```

```
[+] Building 0.9s (7/7) FINISHED
 => [internal] load build definition from Dockerfile  0.0s
 => => transferring dockerfile: 37B 0.0s
 => [internal] load .dockerignore   0.0s
 => => transferring context: 2B   0.0s
 => [internal] load metadata for docker.io/library/
    nginx:alpine   0.8s
 => [internal] load build context   0.0s
 => => transferring context: 34B 0.0s
 => [1/2] FROM docker.io/library/nginx:alpine@
    sha256:ad14f34   0.0s
 => CACHED [2/2] COPY default.conf /etc/nginx/conf.d   0.0s
 => exporting to image  0.0s
 => => exporting layers 0.0s
 => => writing image sha256:f6f3af7 0.0s
 => => naming to docker.io/sathyabhat/nginx-volume 0.0s
```

Before you run this image, look at the custom `nginx default.conf`
contents:

```
server {
    listen        80;
    server_name  localhost;

    location / {
        root    /srv/www/starter;
        index   index.html index.htm;
    }
    access_log  /var/log/nginx/access.log;
    access_log  /var/log/nginx/error.log;

    error_page    500 502 503 504   /50x.html;
    location = /50x.html {
        root    /usr/share/nginx/html;
    }

}
```

The `nginx` config is a simple config; it tells `nginx` to serve a default file
called `index.html` to `/srv/www/starter/`. Let's run the Docker container.
Since `nginx` is listening to port 80, you need to tell Docker to publish the ports
using the -p flag:

```
docker run -d --name nginx-volume  -p 8080:80 sathyabhat/nginx-
volume
```

Note that you are publishing from the Docker host's port 8080 to port
80 of the container. Try to load the web page by navigating to `http://`
`localhost:8080`.

Figure 5-1. A 404 error when the source directory is not mounted

When you load the website, you'll see a HTTP 404 - Page Not Found error (see Figure 5-1). This is because in the nginx config file, you directed nginx to serve index.html. However, you have not yet copied the index.html file to the container and have not mounted the location of the index.html to the container as a bind mount. As a result, nginx cannot find the index.html file.

You can correct this error by copying the website files to the container, as you saw in the previous chapter. In this exercise, you will leverage the bind mount feature you learned about earlier and mount the entire directory containing the sources. All that is needed is to use pass the bind mount flag that you learned about earlier. You don't have to make changes to the Dockerfile.

Stop the existing container using the following command:

```
docker stop nginx-volume
```

Now, start a new container with the bind mount, as shown in the following command:

```
docker run -d --name nginx-volume-bind -v "$(pwd)"/:/srv/www  -p
8080:80 sathyabhat/nginx-volume
```

Confirm that the container is running using the following command:

```
docker ps
```

You should see a list of running containers, as shown here:

```
CONTAINER
ID      IMAGE          COMMAND          CREATED          STATUS
PORTS          NAMES
54c857ca065b     sathyabhat/nginx-volume     "nginx -g 'daemon of..."
6 minutes ago      Up 6 minutes          0.0.0.0:8080->80/tcp
nginx-volume-bind
```

Confirm that the volumes and mounts are correct using this command:

```
docker inspect nginx-volume-bind | jq ".[].Mounts"
[
  {
    "Type": "bind",
    "Source": "/code/practical-docker-with-python/docker-volume-
            bind-mount/",
    "Destination": "/srv/www",
    "Mode": "",
    "RW": true,
    "Propagation": "rprivate"
  },
  {
    "Type": "volume",
    "Name": "c069ba7",
```

```
    "Source": "/var/lib/docker/volumes/c069ba7/_data",
    "Destination": "/var/lib",
    "Driver": "local",
    "Mode": "",
    "RW": true,
    "Propagation": ""
  }
]
```

Let's navigate to the same URL again. If the mounts section looks fine, then you should see the page in Figure 5-2.

Figure 5-2. *nginx serving the web page successfully*

Success!

ADDING VOLUMES TO NEWSBOT

In the previous chapter's exercises, you wrote a Dockerfile for Newsbot. However, as you might have noticed, killing the container resets the state of Newsbot and you need to customize the bot all over again. To fix this, you will add an SQLite database and the data file of this database will be saved to a Docker volume. By completing this exercise, you will know you can persist the data from a container by saving it to a volume and then reattach the volume to a new container.

The Newsbot source code has been slightly modified from the codebase so that the preferences, (i.e., which subreddit the news should be fetched from) are saved to a SQLite database.

Tip   The source code and associated Dockerfile are available on the GitHub repo of this book at `https://github.com/Apress/practical-docker-with-python`, in the `source-code/chapter-5/exercise-2` directory.

The Dockerfile is modified as shown here:

```
FROM python:3-alpine

RUN apk add gcc musl-dev python3-dev libffi-dev openssl-dev
WORKDIR /apps/subredditfetcher/
COPY . .
RUN pip install -r requirements.txt
CMD ["python", "newsbot.py"]
```

In this Dockerfile, you start with `python:3-alpine` as the base image. You add the RUN step to install some library dependencies required for the Python packages. You then copy the source code into the container and install the required Python packages. Another notable change is the addition of the

VOLUME instruction. As you learned earlier, this is to tell Docker to mark the directory specified to be managed as a volume, even if you did not specify the required volume name in the docker run command.

Build the image using the following command:

```
docker build -t sathyabhat/newsbot-sqlite .
```

The build logs are shown here:

```
[+] Building 9.5s (11/11) FINISHED
 => [internal] load build definition from Dockerfile 0.1s
 => => transferring dockerfile: 38B    0.0s
 => [internal] load .dockerignore  0.1s
 => => transferring context: 2B 0.0s
 => [internal] load metadata for docker.io/library/python:3-
    alpine   2.3s
 => [auth] library/python:pull token for registry-1.docker.io 0.0s
 => [internal] load build context   0.1s
 => => transferring context: 6.23kB    0.0s
 => [1/5] FROM docker.io/library/python:3-alpine@sha256:eb31d7f  0.0s
 => CACHED [2/5] RUN apk add gcc musl-dev python3-dev libffi-dev
    openssl-dev 0.0s
 => CACHED [3/5] WORKDIR /apps/subredditfetcher/  0.0s
 => [4/5] COPY . .   0.1s
 => [5/5] RUN pip install -r requirements.txt   6.3s
 => exporting to image 0.4s
 => => exporting layers    0.3s
 => => writing image sha256:6605a7a    0.0s
 => => naming to docker.io/sathyabhat/newsbot-sqlite 0.0s
```

Now run the bot using the docker run command. Note that you provide the volume name via the -v flag. Don't forget to pass the Newsbot API key generated in Chapter 3 to the NBT_ACCESS_TOKEN environment variable.

```
docker run --rm --name newsbot-sqlite -e NBT_ACCESS_TOKEN -v
newsbot-data:/data sathyabhat/newsbot-sqlite
```

The run command creates a new container called newsbot-sqlite, with a volume called newsbot-data attached to the container and mounted to the /data directory inside the container. The --rm flag ensures that the container is removed when it is stopped.

If the bot starts fine, you should start seeing these logs:

```
docker run --rm --name newsbot-sqlite -e NBT_ACCESS_
TOKEN=<token> -v newsbot-data:/data sathyabhat/newsbot-sqlite

INFO: <module> - Starting newsbot
INFO: get_updates - received response: {'ok': True, 'result': []}
INFO: get_updates - received response: {'ok': True, 'result': []}
INFO: get_updates - received response: {'ok': True, 'result': []}
INFO: get_updates - received response: {'ok': True, 'result': []}
```

Try setting a subreddit from which the bot should fetch the data, say Python. To do this, from Telegram, find the bot and type /source python.

The logs from the application should confirm the receipt of the command:

```
INFO: - handle_incoming_messages - Chat text received: /source
        python
INFO: - handle_incoming_messages - Sources set for nnn
        to  python
INFO: - handle_incoming_messages - nnn
INFO: - post_message - posting Sources set as  python! to nnn
```

The Telegram window should now look like Figure 5-3.

Figure 5-3. *Acknowledgement of the subreddit source*

Now you can fetch some content. To do this, type /fetch in the bot window. The application should respond with a loading message and another chat with the contents (see Figure 5-4).

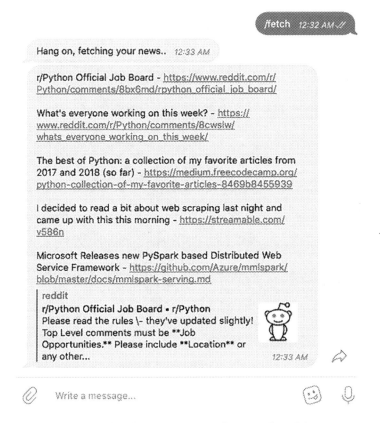

Figure 5-4. *The bot is fetching contents from subreddit*

You can now test for data persistency by stopping the bot, removing the container, and creating a new container. First stop Newsbot by pressing Ctrl+C. Since you started the container using the --rm flag, Docker will automatically remove the container. Create a new container by typing the same command you used previously to launch the container:

```
docker run --rm --name newsbot-sqlite -e NBT_ACCESS_TOKEN -v
newsbot-data:/data sathyabhat/newsbot-sqlite
```

Now, in the Telegram chat window, type /fetch again. Since the subreddit source has been saved to the database, you should see the content from the previously configured subreddit (see Figure 5-5).

Figure 5-5. *Newsbot fetching contents from subreddit after removing and starting a new container*

Look at the content again—the Docker volume setup is working correctly. Congrats! You have successfully set up data persistence for this project.

Summary

In this chapter, you learned why data persistence is a problem in containers and the different strategies Docker offers for managing data persistence. You also took a deep dive into configuring *volumes* and learned how they differ from *bind mounts*. Finally, you ran some hands-on exercises on how to work with bind mounts and volumes and added volumes support for Newsbot. In the next chapter, you will learn more about Docker networking and learn how containers can connect to each other.

CHAPTER 6

Understanding Docker Networks

In the previous chapters, you learned about Docker and its associated terminologies, took a deeper look into how to build Docker images using the Dockerfile, and learned about how to persist data generated by containers.

In this chapter, you will look at networking in Docker and learn how containers can talk to each other and discover each other with the help of Docker's networking features.

Why Do We Need Container Networking?

Traditionally, most compute solutions are thought of as single-purpose solutions—it is not often that you come across a single host (or a Virtual Machine) hosting multiple workloads—especially production workloads. With containers, the scenario changes. With lightweight containers and the presence of advanced orchestration platforms such as Kubernetes and DC/OS, it is very common to have multiple containers of different workloads running on the same host with different instances of the application distributed across multiple hosts. In such cases, container networking helps in allowing (or limiting) cross-container talk. And to facilitate this process, Docker comes with different modes of networks.

© Sathyajith Bhat 2022
S. Bhat, *Practical Docker with Python*, https://doi.org/10.1007/978-1-4842-7815-4_6

Tip Docker's networking subsystem is implemented by pluggable drivers; Docker comes with four drivers out of the box, with more drivers being available from Docker Store, available at `https://store.docker.com/search?category=network&q=&type=plugin`.

It is important to note that all of Docker's networking modes are achieved via *Software Defined Networking* (SDN). Specifically, on Linux systems, Docker modifies iptables rules to provide the required level of access/isolation.

Default Docker Network Drivers

With a standard install of Docker, the following network drivers are available:

- Bridge
- Host
- Overlay
- Macvlan
- None

Bridge Networks

A *bridge* network is a user-defined network that allows for all containers connected on the same network to communicate with each other. The benefit is that the containers on the same bridge network can connect, discover, and talk to each other while those not on the same bridge cannot communicate directly. Bridge networks are useful when you have containers running on the same host that need to talk to each other—if the containers that need to communicate are on different Docker hosts, then an overlay network is needed.

When Docker is installed and started, a default bridge network is created and newly started containers connect to it. However, it is always better if you create a bridge network yourself. The reasons are multiple:

- **Better isolation across containers.** As you learned, containers on the same bridge network are discoverable and can talk to each other. They automatically expose all ports to each other, and no ports are exposed to the outside world. Having a separate user-defined bridged network for each application provides better isolation between containers of different applications.

- **Easy name resolution across containers.** For services joining the same bridged network, containers can connect to each other by name. For containers on the default bridged network, the only way for containers to connect to each other is via IP addresses or by using the `--link` flag, which has been deprecated.

- **Easy attachment/detachment of containers on user-defined networks.** For containers on the default network, the only way to detach them is to stop the running container and re-create it on the new network.

Host Networks

As the name suggests, with a host network, a container is attached to the Docker host. This means that any traffic coming to the host is routed to the container. Since all of container's ports are directly attached to the host, in this mode, the concept of publishing ports doesn't make sense. Host mode is perfect when you have only one container running on the Docker host.

Overlay Networks

Overlay networks create a network spanning multiple docker hosts. This type of network is called an overlay because it lays on top of the existing host network, allowing containers connected to the overlay network to communicate across multiple hosts. Overlay networks are an advanced topic and are primarily used when a cluster of Docker hosts is set up in Swarm mode. Overlay networks also let you encrypt the application data traffic across the them.

Macvlan Networks

Macvlan networks leverage the Linux Kernel's ability to assign multiple logical addresses based on MAC to a single physical interface. This means that you can assign a MAC address to a container's virtual network interface, making it appear as if the container has a physical network interface connected to the network. This brings unique opportunities, especially for legacy applications that expect a physical interface to be present and connected to the physical network.

Macvlan networks require an additional dependency on the *Network Interface Card* (NIC) to support what is known as "promiscuous" mode—a special mode that allows the NIC to receive all traffic and direct it to a controller, instead of receiving only traffic that the NIC expects to receive.

None Networking

When a container is launched, Docker connects the container to the default bridge network. The bridge network allows the container to make outgoing network requests. Although container networking is definitely a feature and highlight, there are many cases where an application must be completely isolated and must not allow for incoming or outgoing requests—especially with high security and compliance requirement applications. In such cases, a none networking comes in handy.

As the name suggests, none networking is when the container isn't connected to any network interface and does not receive or send any network traffic. In this networking mode, only the loopback interface is created, allowing the container to talk to itself, but not to the outside world or with other containers.

A container can be launched with none networking using the command shown here:

```
docker run -d --name nginx --network=none -p 80:80 nginx
```

Trying to `curl` the endpoint results in an instant `Connection Refused`, indicating that the container is not accepting connections.

```
curl localhost
curl: (7) Failed to connect to localhost port 80 after 1 ms:
Connection refused
```

If you open an interactive terminal with the container and try an outgoing network request using `curl`, as shown here:

```
docker exec -it nginx sh
curl google.com
curl: (6) Could not resolve host: google.com
```

You'll see that there is no networking configured. The container cannot receive or send network traffic.

Working with Docker Networks

Now that you conceptually understand the different network modes, you can try some of them. This chapter only looks at the bridge network, as it's the most commonly used driver. Much like the other subsystems, Docker comes with a subcommand for handling Docker networks. To get started, try the following command:

```
docker network
```

You should see an explanation of the available options:

```
docker network

Usage:   docker network COMMAND

Manage networks

Options:

Commands:
  connect      Connect a container to a network
  create       Create a network
  disconnect   Disconnect a container from a network
  inspect      Display detailed information on one or more networks
  ls           List networks
  prune        Remove all unused networks
  rm           Remove one or more networks
```

Now look at which networks are available. To do this, type the following:

```
docker network ls
```

At the minimum, you should see these networks listed:

```
docker network ls
NETWORK ID NAME DRIVER SCOPE
8ea951d9f963 bridge bridge local
790ed54b21ee host host local
38ce4d23e021 none null local
```

Each of these corresponds to the three different types of networks mentioned previously—the bridge, the host, and the none type of networks. You can examine the details of the networking by typing the following:

```
docker network inspect <network id or name>
```

For instance, if you want to check the default bridge network, type the following command:

```
docker network inspect bridge
[
    {
        "Name": "bridge",
        "Id": "c540708",
        "Created": "2018-04-17T13:10:43.002552762Z",
        "Scope": "local",
        "Driver": "bridge",
        "EnableIPv6": false,
        "IPAM": {
            "Driver": "default",
            "Options": null,
            "Config": [
                {
                    "Subnet": "172.17.0.0/16",
                    "Gateway": "172.17.0.1"
                }
            ]
        },
        "Internal": false,
        "Attachable": false,
        "Ingress": false,
        "ConfigFrom": {
            "Network": ""
        },
        "ConfigOnly": false,
        "Containers": {},
        "Options": {
            "com.docker.network.bridge.default_bridge": "true",
```

```
        "com.docker.network.bridge.enable_icc": "true",
        "com.docker.network.bridge.enable_ip_masquerade":
        "true",
        "com.docker.network.bridge.host_binding_ipv4":
        "0.0.0.0",
        "com.docker.network.bridge.name": "docker0",
        "com.docker.network.driver.mtu": "1500"
    },
    "Labels": {}
  }
]
```

Among other things, you can see that:

- The com.docker.network.bridge.default_bridge key under Options indicates that the bridge is the default.

- "EnableIPv6": false indicates that IPv6 is disabled for this bridge.

- The "Subnet" key under IPAM - Config indicates that the Docker network subnet has a CIDR of 172.17.0.0/16. This means that up to 65,536 containers can be attached to this network (this is derived from the CIDR block of /16).

- The com.docker.network.bridge.enable_ip_ masquerade under Options indicates that the bridge has IP masquerading enabled. This means that the outside world cannot see the container's private IP and it will appear as if the requests are coming from the Docker host.

- The com.docker.network.bridge.host_binding_ipv4 indicates that the host binding is 0.0.0.0. This that the bridge is bound to all interfaces on the host.

In contrast, if you inspect the none network:

```
docker network inspect none
[
    {
        "Name": "none",
        "Id": "d30afbe",
        "Created": "2017-05-10T10:37:04.125762206Z",
        "Scope": "local",
        "Driver": "null",
        "EnableIPv6": false,
        "IPAM": {
            "Driver": "default",
            "Options": null,
            "Config": []
        },
        "Internal": false,
        "Attachable": false,
        "Ingress": false,
        "ConfigFrom": {
            "Network": ""
        },
        "ConfigOnly": false,
        "Containers": {},
        "Options": {},
        "Labels": {}
    }
]
```

The driver null indicates that no networking will be handled for this.

Bridge Networks

Before you create a bridge network, you need to create two containers running:

- MySQL database server
- adminer, a web-based portal for managing MySQL databases

To create the MySQL container, run the following command:

```
docker run -d --name mysql -p 3306:3306 -e MYSQL_ROOT_
PASSWORD=dontusethisinprod mysql:8
```

Since you are starting in detached mode (as specified by the -d flag), follow the logs until you are certain the container is up:

```
docker logs -f mysql
```

The result should be the following lines:

```
Initializing database
[...]
Database initialized
[...]
MySQL init process in progress...
[...]
MySQL init process done. Ready for start-up.
[...]
[Note] mysqld: ready for connections.
Version: '8.0.26'  socket: '/var/run/mysqld/mysqld.sock'  port:
3306  MySQL Community Server (GPL)
[...]
```

If you see the last set of lines, the MySQL database container is ready. Create the adminer container:

```
docker run -d --name adminer -p 8080:8080 adminer
```

Here are the logs of adminer:

```
docker logs -f adminer
PHP 7.4.22 Development Server started
```

That means adminer is ready. Now look at the two containers—specifically, their networking aspects.

```
docker inspect mysql | jq ".[0].NetworkSettings.Networks"
{
  "bridge": {
    "IPAMConfig": null,
    "Links": null,
    "Aliases": null,
    "NetworkID": "8ea951d",
    "EndpointID": "c33e38",
    "Gateway": "172.17.0.1",
    "IPAddress": "172.17.0.2",
    "IPPrefixLen": 16,
    "IPv6Gateway": "",
    "GlobalIPv6Address": "",
    "GlobalIPv6PrefixLen": 0,
    "MacAddress": "02:42:ac:11:00:03",
    "DriverOpts": null
  }
}
```

From this output, you know that the MySQL container has been assigned an IP address of 172.17.0.2 on the default bridge network. Now examine the adminer container:

```
docker inspect adminer | jq ".[0].NetworkSettings.Networks"
{
  "bridge": {
    "IPAMConfig": null,
    "Links": null,
    "Aliases": null,
    "NetworkID": "8ea951d",
    "EndpointID": "a26bcc",
    "Gateway": "172.17.0.1",
    "IPAddress": "172.17.0.3",
    "IPPrefixLen": 16,
    "IPv6Gateway": "",
    "GlobalIPv6Address": "",
    "GlobalIPv6PrefixLen": 0,
    "MacAddress": "02:42:ac:11:00:04",
    "DriverOpts": null
  }
}
```

The adminer container is associated with IP address of 172.17.0.3 within the bridge network. However, since both containers are bound to the host IP of 0.0.0.0, translated to all interfaces of the Docker host, you should be able to connect by its port.

Within a bridge network, whether it's the default Docker bridge network or a custom bridge network that you create (you will see this in the chapter's exercise), all the containers are accessible using *their container names*. However, these containers can be accessed from the host only if their ports have been exposed. To demonstrate this, try to connect to the database via adminer. Navigate to http://localhost:8080.

Enter the server as mysql and try to log in. You'll notice that the login will fail (see Figure 6-1).

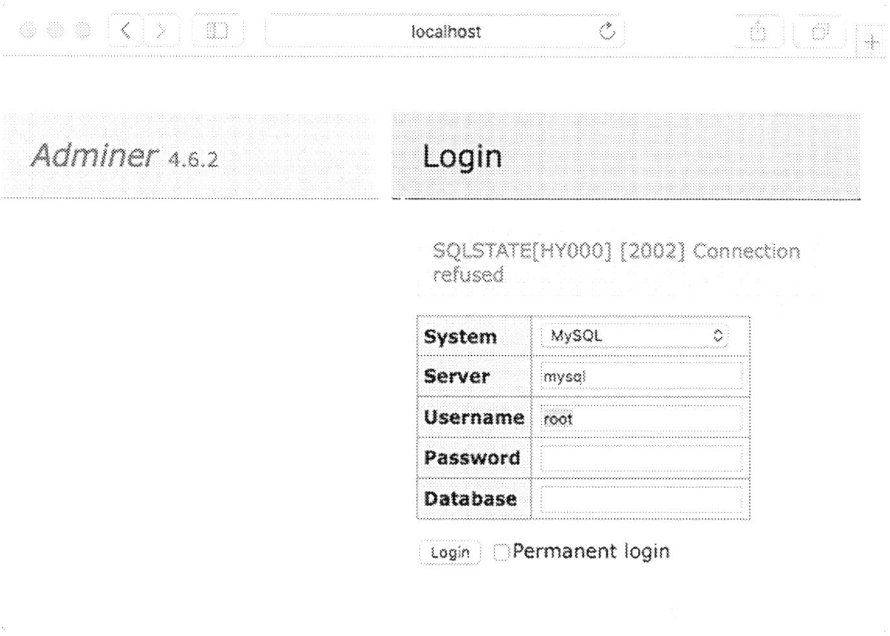

Figure 6-1. *Connection to named host fails*

Try to log in again, this time in the server box. Enter the IP address of the MySQL container, as shown in Figure 6-2.

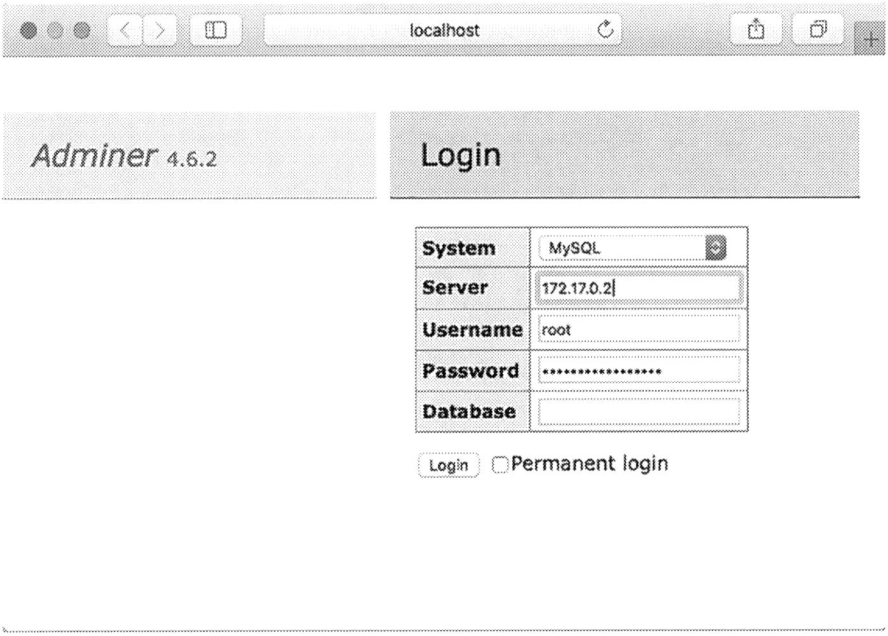

Figure 6-2. Trying to log in with the IP address of the container

When you try to log in, it should be successful (see Figure 6-3).

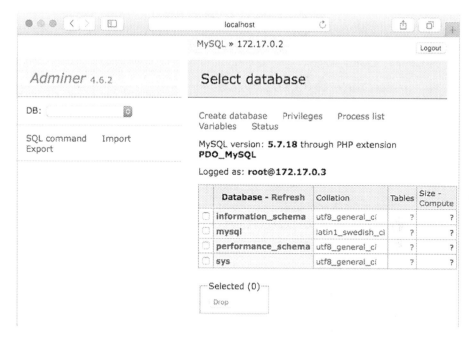

Figure 6-3. *Login with IP address is successful*

The login is successful. While entering the IP is an acceptable workaround when there's only one dependent container, many applications have multiple dependencies. This approach breaks down in those cases.

Creating Named Bridge Networks

In this section, you'll create a database network and try to connect the MySQL and the `adminer` container to the network. You can create a bridge network by typing the following command:

```
docker network create <network name>
```

Docker gives you more options in terms of specifying the subnet, but for most part the defaults are good. Note that the bridge network allows you to create only a single subnet.

Create a network called database using the following command:

```
docker network create database
```

Now inspect the network you created:

```
docker network inspect database
[
    {
        "Name": "database",
        "Id": "8574145",
        "Created": "2021-07-31T15:58:11.4652433Z",
        "Scope": "local",
        "Driver": "bridge",
        "EnableIPv6": false,
        "IPAM": {
            "Driver": "default",
            "Options": {},
            "Config": [
                {
                    "Subnet": "172.18.0.0/16",
                    "Gateway": "172.18.0.1"
                }
            ]
        },
        "Internal": false,
        "Attachable": false,
        "Ingress": false,
        "ConfigFrom": {
            "Network": ""
        },
        "ConfigOnly": false,
        "Containers": {},
```

```
        "Options": {},
        "Labels": {}
    }
]
```

Note that the created network has a subnet of `172.18.0.0/16.` Stop and remove the existing containers using the following commands:

```
docker stop adminer
docker rm adminer
docker stop mysql
docker rm mysql
```

Now launch the MySQL container, this time connected to the database network. The command is as follows:

```
docker run -d --network database --name mysql -p 3306:3306 -e
MYSQL_ROOT_PASSWORD=dontusethisinprod mysql:8
```

Note the additional `--network` flag, which tells Docker what network it should attach the container to. Wait for the container to initialize. You can also check the logs and ensure that container is ready:

```
docker logs -f mysql
```

The result should be the following lines:

```
Initializing database
[...]
Database initialized
[...]
MySQL init process in progress...
[...]
MySQL init process done. Ready for start up.
[...]
```

```
[Note] mysqld: ready for connections.
Version: '8.0.26'  socket: '/var/run/mysqld/mysqld.sock'  port:
3306  MySQL Community Server (GPL)
[...]
```

Examine the container now:

```
docker inspect mysql | jq ".[0].NetworkSettings.Networks"
{
  "database": {
    "IPAMConfig": null,
    "Links": null,
    "Aliases": [
      "6149cb2453da"
    ],
    "NetworkID": "8574145",
    "EndpointID": "3343960402",
    "Gateway": "172.18.0.1",
    "IPAddress": "172.18.0.2",
    "IPPrefixLen": 16,
    "IPv6Gateway": "",
    "GlobalIPv6Address": "",
    "GlobalIPv6PrefixLen": 0,
    "MacAddress": "02:42:ac:12:00:02",
    "DriverOpts": null
  }
}
```

Note that the container is part of the database network. You can confirm this by inspecting the database network as well.

```
docker network inspect database | jq ".[0].Containers"
{
  "6149cb2": {
    "Name": "mysql",
    "EndpointID": "3343960",
    "MacAddress": "02:42:ac:12:00:02",
    "IPv4Address": "172.18.0.2/16",
    "IPv6Address": ""
  }
}
```

Note that the containers key in the database network has the MySQL container. Launch the adminer container as well. Type the following command:

```
docker run -d --name adminer -p 8080:8080 adminer
```

Notice that the --network command has been omitted. This means adminer will be connected to the default bridge network:

```
docker inspect adminer | jq ".[0].NetworkSettings.Networks"
{
  "bridge": {
    "IPAMConfig": null,
    "Links": null,
    "Aliases": null,
    "NetworkID": "8ea951d",
    "EndpointID": "c1a5df0",
    "Gateway": "172.17.0.1",
    "IPAddress": "172.17.0.2",
    "IPPrefixLen": 16,
    "IPv6Gateway": "",
    "GlobalIPv6Address": "",
```

```
    "GlobalIPv6PrefixLen": 0,
    "MacAddress": "02:42:ac:11:00:02",
    "DriverOpts": null
  }
}
```

Connecting Containers to Named Bridge Networks

Docker lets you easily connect a container to another network on the fly.
To do this, type the following command:

```
dockr network connect <network name> <container name>
```

You need to connect the adminer container to the database network, as
follows:

```
docker network connect database adminer
```

Inspect the adminer container now:

```
docker inspect adminer | jq ".[0].NetworkSettings.Networks"
{
  "bridge": {
    "IPAMConfig": null,
    "Links": null,
    "Aliases": null,
    "NetworkID": "8ea951d",
[...]
    "DriverOpts": null
  },
  "database": {
    "IPAMConfig": {},
    "Links": null,
    "Aliases": [
```

```
      "2a7363ec1888"
    ],
    "NetworkID": "8574145",
    [...]
    "DriverOpts": {}
  }
}
```

Notice that the networks key has two networks, the default bridge network and the database network that you just connected to. Since the container doesn't need to be connected to the default bridge network, you can disconnect it. To do this, the command is as follows:

```
docker network disconnect bridge adminer
```

Examining the adminer container now using the following command, you can see only the database network connected.

```
docker inspect adminer | jq ".[0].NetworkSettings.Networks"
{
  "database": {
    "IPAMConfig": {},
    "Links": null,
    "Aliases": [
      "2a7363ec1888"
    ],
    "NetworkID": "8574145",
[...]
    "DriverOpts": {}
  }
}
```

The bridge network is no longer attached to the `adminer` network. Launch `adminer` by navigating to `http://localhost:8080`. In the Server field, type the name of the container that you want to connect to, that is, the database container name, `mysql`, as shown in Figure 6-4.

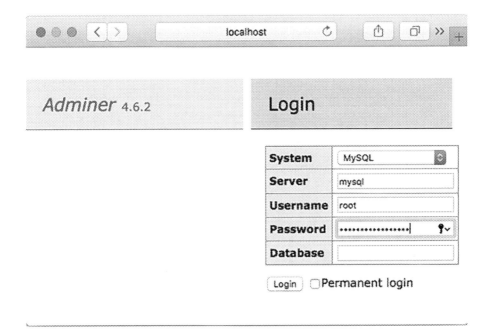

Figure 6-4. *Connecting to container via named host*

Enter the details and click Login. The login should be successful, and you should see a screen like the one shown in Figure 6-5.

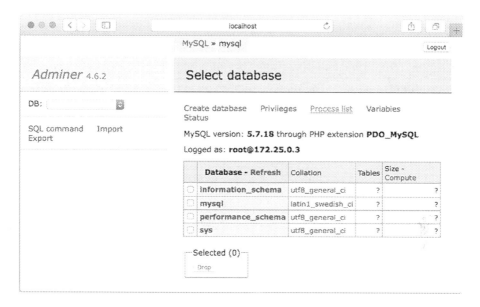

Figure 6-5. *Named host resolves to IP and connects successfully*

Thus, user-defined bridged networks make connecting services very easy; you don't have to mess and search for the IP addresses. Docker makes it easy by letting you connect to the services using the name of the container as the host. Docker handles the behind-the-scenes translation of the container name to the IP address.

Host Networks

In a host network, Docker doesn't create a virtual network for the container; rather, the Docker host's network interface is bound to the container.

Host networks are excellent when you have only one container running on the host and don't need any bridge networks or network isolation. Now you'll create a nginx container running in host mode to see how you can run it.

Earlier you saw that there is already a network called host. This is not the name that governs whether the network is a host network; it's the driver. Recall that the host network has a host driver, and hence any container connected to the host network will run in host network mode.

To start the container, you simply pass the --network host parameter. Try the following command to start a nginx container and publish port 80 of the container to the host's 8080 port.

```
docker run -d --network host -p 8080:80 nginx:alpine
WARNING: Published ports are discarded when using host network mode
```

Notice that Docker warns you that port publishing isn't being used. Since the container's ports are directly bound to the Docker post, the concept of a published port doesn't arise. The actual command should be as follows:

```
docker run -d --network host nginx:alpine
```

Exercises

CONNECTING A MYSQL CONTAINER TO A NEWSBOT CONTAINER

In the previous chapter's exercises, you wrote a Dockerfile for Newsbot and built the container. You then used Docker volumes to persist the database across containers. In this exercise, you will modify Newsbot so that the data persists to a MySQL database, instead of being saved to an SQLite DB. You will then create a custom bridge network to connect the project container and the MySQL container.

Tip   The source code and associated Dockerfile are available on the GitHub repo of this book at https://github.com/Apress/ practical-docker-with-python, in the source-code/ chapter-6/exercise-1 directory.

Consider the following Dockerfile. It looks, and actually is, quite similar to
the Dockerfile you used in Exercise 2 of Chapter 5. The only change that is
needed is to Newsbot's code so that it connects to the MySQL server instead
of reading from the SQLite database.

```
FROM python:3-alpine

RUN apk add gcc musl-dev python3-dev libffi-dev openssl-dev
WORKDIR /apps/subredditfetcher/
COPY . .
RUN pip install -r requirements.txt
CMD ["python", "newsbot.py"]
```

Now build the container using the following command:

```
docker build -t sathyabhat/newsbot-mysql .
[+] Building 2.9s (11/11) FINISHED
 => [internal] load build definition from Dockerfile    0.1s
 => => transferring dockerfile: 38B  0.0s
 => [internal] load .dockerignore 0.1s
 => => transferring context: 2B    0.0s
 => [internal] load metadata for docker.io/library/python:3-
    alpine 2.6s
 => [auth] library/python:pull token for registry-1.docker.io    0.0s
 => [1/5] FROM docker.io/library/python:3-alpine@sha256:1e8728b 0.0s
 => => resolve docker.io/library/python:3-alpine@sha256:1e8728b 0.0s
 => [internal] load build context 0.0s
 => => transferring context: 309B 0.0s
 => CACHED [2/5] RUN apk add gcc musl-dev python3-dev libffi-dev
    openssl-dev cargo    0.0s
 => CACHED [3/5] WORKDIR /apps/subredditfetcher/ 0.0s
 => CACHED [4/5] COPY . .    0.0s
 => CACHED [5/5] RUN pip install --upgrade pip && pip install -r
    requirements.txt 0.0s
 => exporting to image    0.0s
```

```
=> => exporting layers   0.0s
=> => writing image sha256:44cd813   0.0s
=> => naming to docker.io/sathyabhat/newsbot-mysql 0.0s
```

Create a new network called newsbot to which the containers will be
connected. To do this, type the following:

```
docker network create newsbot
```

Now you'll bring up a new MySQL container and connect it to the network you
created previously. Since you want the data to persist, you will also mount the
MySQL database to a volume called newsbot-db. This exercise uses root for
the username and dontusethisinprod for the password. These credentials
are extremely weak and we highly recommend you not use them in the real
world.

Type the following command to start the MySQL container:

```
docker run -d --name mysql --network newsbot -v newsbot-db:/var/
lib/mysql -e MYSQL_ROOT_PASSWORD=dontusethisinprod mysql:8
```

Note the --network flag, which tells Docker to connect the mysql container
to the network called newsbot. MySQL saves all files related to the database
in the /var/lib/mysql directory, and the -v newsbot-db:/var/lib/
mysql flag instructs Docker to save the contents of the /var/lib/mysql
directory in the container to the volume called newsbot-db. That way, the
contents are persisted even after the container has been removed.

Follow the logs and verify that the MySQL database is up:

```
docker logs mysql

Initializing database
[...]
Database initialized
[...]
```

```
MySQL init process in progress
[...]
MySQL init process done. Ready for start up.
[...]
2021-08-01T12:41:15.295013Z 0 [Note] mysqld: ready for
connections.
Version: '8.0.26'  socket: '/var/run/mysqld/mysqld.sock'  port:
3306  MySQL Community Server (GPL)
```

The last couple of lines indicate that the MySQL database is up. Now start the Newsbot container while connecting it to the newsbot network that you created. To do this, type the following command:

```
docker run --rm --network newsbot --name newsbot-mysql -e NBT_
ACCESS_TOKEN=<token> sathyabhat/newsbot-mysql
```

Take care to replace <token> with the value of the Newsbot API key generated in Chapter 3.

You should see the following logs:

```
INFO: <module> - Starting up
INFO: <module> - Waiting for 60 seconds for db to come up
INFO: <module> - Checking on dbs
INFO: get_updates - received response: {'ok': True, 'result': []}
INFO: get_updates - received response: {'ok': True, 'result': []}
```

Since created a new volume, the sources that were set from the previous chapter are not available.

Set the subreddit again from which the bot should fetch the data, say Docker. To do this, from Telegram, find the bot and type /source docker. The logs from the application should confirm the receipt of the command:

```
INFO: handle_incoming_messages - Chat text received: /source
      docker
INFO: handle_incoming_messages - Sources set for 7342383
      to  docker
INFO: handle_incoming_messages - 7342383
INFO: post_message - posting Sources set as  docker! to 7342383
INFO: get_updates - received response: {'ok': True, 'result': []}
INFO: get_updates - received response: {'ok': True, 'result': []}
INFO: get_updates - received response: {'ok': True, 'result': []}
INFO: get_updates - received response: {'ok': True, 'result': []}
```

Your Telegram window should look like the one shown in Figure 6-6.

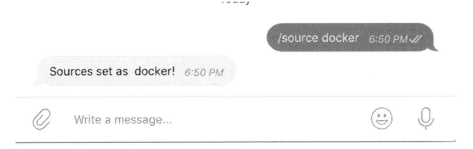

Figure 6-6. *Acknowledgement of the subreddit source*

Now you can fetch some content. To do this, type /fetch in the bot window. The application should respond by loading a message and another chat with the contents, as shown in Figure 6-7.

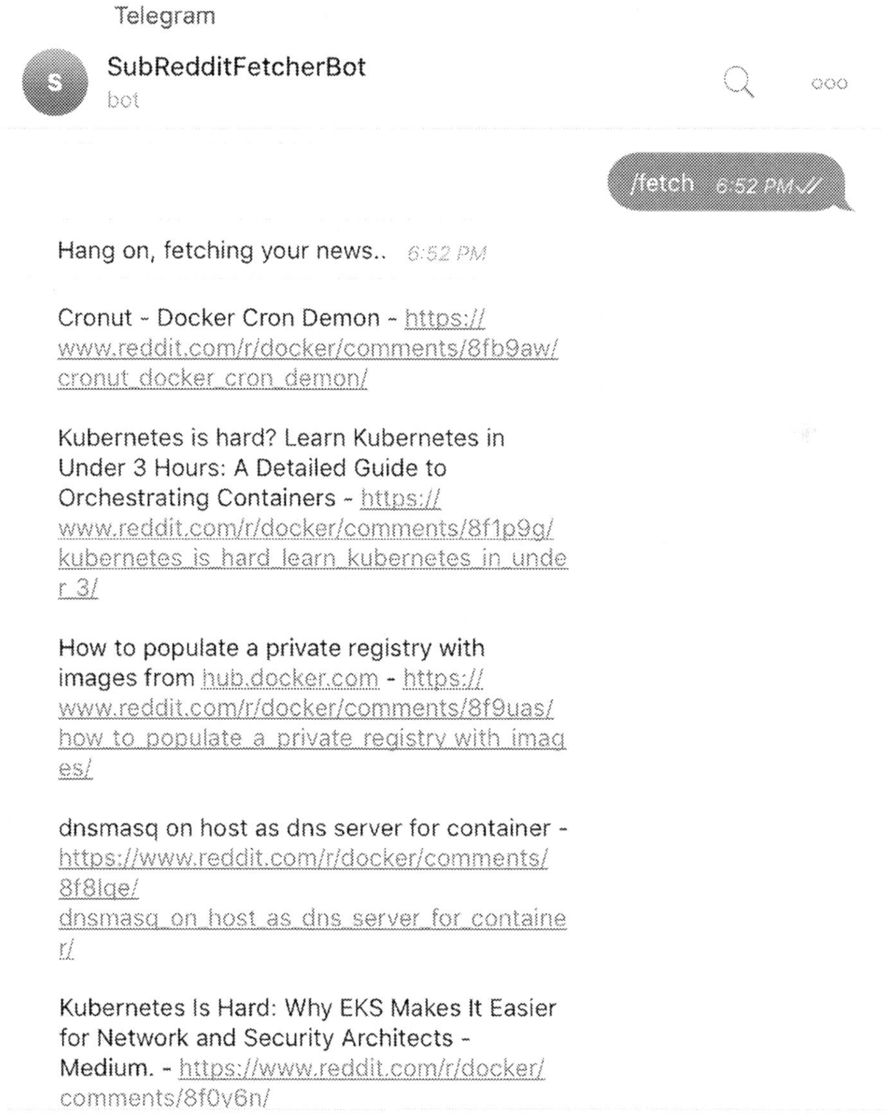

Telegram

SubRedditFetcherBot
bot

/fetch 6:52 PM ✓✓

Hang on, fetching your news.. 6:52 PM

Cronut - Docker Cron Demon - https://
www.reddit.com/r/docker/comments/8fb9aw/
cronut_docker_cron_demon/

Kubernetes is hard? Learn Kubernetes in
Under 3 Hours: A Detailed Guide to
Orchestrating Containers - https://
www.reddit.com/r/docker/comments/8f1p9g/
kubernetes_is_hard_learn_kubernetes_in_unde
r_3/

How to populate a private registry with
images from hub.docker.com - https://
www.reddit.com/r/docker/comments/8f9uas/
how_to_populate_a_private_registry_with_imag
es/

dnsmasq on host as dns server for container -
https://www.reddit.com/r/docker/comments/
8f8lqe/
dnsmasq_on_host_as_dns_server_for_containe
r/

Kubernetes Is Hard: Why EKS Makes It Easier
for Network and Security Architects -
Medium. - https://www.reddit.com/r/docker/
comments/8f0y6n/

Figure 6-7. *The bot is fetching contents from the subreddit*

Now you'll confirm that Newsbot is indeed saving the sources to the database. To do this, connect to the running `mysql` container using the following command:

```
docker exec --it mysql sh
```

Now in the container shell, type the following command to connect to the MySQL server:

```
mysql -p
```

Enter the password (mentioned previously) to connect. You'll get the following message if you entered the correct password:

```
Welcome to the MySQL monitor.  Commands end with ; or \g.
Your MySQL connection id is 32
Server version: 8.0.26 MySQL Community Server - GPL
Copyright (c) 2000, 2021, Oracle and/or its affiliates.
Oracle is a registered trademark of Oracle Corporation and/or its
affiliates. Other names may be trademarks of their respective
owners.
Type 'help;' or '\h' for help. Type '\c' to clear the current
input statement.
mysql>
```

In the MySQL prompt, type the following command to ensure that the Newsbot database exists:

```
show databases;
```

You should see a database list similar to the following listing:

```
show databases;
+--------------------+
| Database           |
+--------------------+
| information_schema |
| mysql              |
| newsbot            |
| performance_schema |
| sys                |
+--------------------+
5 rows in set (0.03 sec)
```

Type the following command to select the database and then fetch the contents of the table called source:

```
use newsbot
select * from source;
+-----------+------------+
| person_id | fetch_from |
+-----------+------------+
|   7342383 |   docker   |
+-----------+------------+
1 row in set (0.00 sec)
```

This shows you that Newsbot can successfully connect to the MySQL container and save data to the database.

Summary

In this chapter, you learned about the basics of container networking and the different modes of Docker networking. You also learned how to create and work with custom Docker bridged networks and read about insights into Docker host networks. Finally, you ran some hands-on exercises on creating a separate Database container (using MySQL) and learned how to connect the Database container to the Newsbot project. In the next chapter, you learn about Docker Compose and how easy Docker Compose makes it to run multiple, dependent containers.

CHAPTER 7

Understanding Docker Compose

In the previous chapters, you learned about Docker and its associated terminologies, took a deeper look into how you can build Docker images using the Dockerfile, understood how to persist data generated by containers, and linked various running containers with the help of Docker's network features.

In this chapter, you will look at Docker Compose, which is a tool for running multi-container applications, bringing up various linked, dependent containers, and more—and all with just one config file and a command.

Overview of Docker Compose

As software becomes more complicated and as you move more toward the microservices architecture, the number of components that need to be deployed increases considerably as well. While microservices might help keep the overall system fluid by encouraging loosely coupled services, from an operations point of view, things get more complicated. This is especially challenging when you have dependent applications. For instance, for a web application to start working correctly, it needs its database to be working before the web tier can start responding to requests.

Docker makes it easy to tie each microservice to a container. Docker Compose makes orchestration of all of these containers very easy. Without Docker Compose, the container orchestration steps would involve building the various images, creating the required networks, and then running the application using a series of `docker run` commands in the necessary order. As and when the number of containers increases and as the deployment targets increase, running these steps manually becomes unreasonable and you will need to go toward automation.

From a local development point of view, bringing up multiple, linked services manually gets very tedious and painful. Docker Compose simplifies this a lot. By just providing a YAML file describing the containers required and the relationship between the containers, Docker Compose lets you bring up all the containers with a single command. And it's not just about bringing up the containers—Docker Compose also lets you do the following:

- Build, stop, and start the containers associated with the application.

- Tail the logs of the running containers, saving you the trouble of having to open multiple terminal sessions for each container.

- View the status of each container.

Docker Compose helps you enable Continuous Integration. By providing multiple, disposable, reproducible environments, Docker Compose lets you run integration tests in isolation, allowing for a clean-room approach to these automated test cases. It lets you run the tests, validate the results, and then tear down the environment cleanly.

Installing Docker Compose

Docker Compose comes pre-installed as part of Docker Install and doesn't require any additional steps to get started on macOS and Windows systems. On Linux systems, you can download the Docker Compose binary from its GitHub Release page, available at https://github.com/docker/compose/releases. Alternatively, you can run the following curl command to download the correct binary.

```
sudo curl -L https://github.com/docker/compose/releases/
download/1.21.0/docker-compose-$(uname -s)-$(uname -m) -o /usr/
local/bin/docker-compose
```

If you have Python and pip installed, you can also use pip to install docker-compose using the following command:

```
pip install docker-compose
```

Note   Ensure that the version number in the pip install docker-compose command matches the latest version of Docker Compose on the GitHub Releases page. Otherwise, you will end up with an outdated version.

Once the binary has been downloaded, change the permissions so that it can be executed using the following command:

```
sudo chmod +x /usr/local/bin/docker-compose
```

If the file was downloaded manually, copy the downloaded file to the /usr/local/bin directory before running the command. To confirm that the install was successful and is working correctly, run the following command:

```
docker-compose version
```

The result should be versions of Docker Compose, something similar to this:

```
docker-compose version 1.29.1, build 5becea4c
docker-py version: 5.0.0
CPython version: 3.9.0
OpenSSL version: OpenSSL 1.1.1g 21 Apr 2020
```

Docker Compose Basics

Unlike the Dockerfile, which is a set of instructions to the Docker Engine about how to build the Docker image, the Compose file is a YAML configuration file that defines the services, networks, and volumes that are required for the application to be started. Docker expects the Compose file to be present in the same path where the docker-compose command is invoked and to be called docker-compose.yaml (or docker-compose. yml). This can be overridden using the -f flag followed by the path to the Compose filename.

Docker Compose Version Overview

With Docker Desktop version 3.4, Docker introduced a newer version of Docker Compose, known as Compose V2. Compose V2 is supposed to be a drop-in replacement for the older version of compose. Docker extracted the YAML file model of the Compose file, created a community around it, and submitted it as a specification, known as the Compose specification. Compose V2 implements the Compose specification. However, it is not yet at feature parity with Compose V1 and can be enabled from within Experimental Settings of Docker Desktop settings. Given the lack of feature parity, this chapter focuses on Compose V1. If you need specific features that are present in Compose V2, such as support for GPU devices and profiles, you can use the rest of the chapter as a guide. Just replace the `docker-compose` command (with the hyphen) with `docker compose` (replace the hyphen with a space) and the commands should still work.

Compose File Versioning and the Compose Spec

Although the Compose file is a YAML file, Docker uses the version key at the start of the file to determine which features of the Docker Engine are supported. There are three versions of the Compose file format. With Docker Compose v1.27.0 and Docker Compose V2, Docker has unified the version 2.x and 3.x of the Compose file format and submitted it to the Community as a specification. Here's a brief description of the previous three versions of the Compose file format:

- **Version 1:** Version 1 is considered a legacy format. If a Docker Compose file doesn't have a version key at the start of the YAML file, Docker considers it to be a version 1 format. Version 1 has been deprecated and is no longer supported.

- **Version 2.x:** Version 2.x identified by the version 2.x key at the start of the YAML file.

- **Version 3.x:** Version 3.x identified by the version 3.x key at the start of the YAML file.

- **Compose spec:** The compose spec unifies versions 2.x and 3.x of the Compose file format and has been submitted it to the Community as a specification. The Compose specification also deprecates the version key.

The differences between the three major versions are discussed in the following sections.

Version 1

Docker Compose files that do not have a version key at the root of the YAML file are considered to be Version 1 compose files. Version 1 will be deprecated and removed in a future version of Docker Compose, so I do not recommend writing Version 1 files. Besides the deprecation, Version 1 has the following major drawbacks:

- Version 1 files cannot declare named services, volumes, or build arguments.

- Container discovery is enabled only by using the links flag.

Version 2

Docker Compose Version 2 files have a version key with a value of 2 or 2.x. Version 2 introduces a few changes, which makes version 2 incompatible with previous versions of Compose files. These include:

- All services must be present in the services key.

- All containers are located on an application-specific default network and the containers can be discovered by the hostname, which is specified by the service name.

- Links are made redundant.

- The depends_on flag is introduced allowing for you to specify dependent containers and the order in which the containers are brought up.

Version 3

Docker Compose Version 3 files have a version key with a value 3 or
3.x. Version 3 removes several options that were deprecated, including
`volume_driver`, `volumes_from`, and many more. Version 3 also adds a
`deploy` key, which is used for deployment and running of services on
Docker Swarm.

Compose Specification

Docker unified versions 2.x and 3.x of the Compose file format and
introduced the Compose specification. With Docker Compose version 1.27
and above, Docker implements the Compose spec as the current latest
format. Docker has also declared the previous versions as legacy, although
they are still supported. The Compose Specification also deprecates the
version key in the Compose file. The Compose Specification allows you
to define container applications not tied to any specific Cloud provider,
comprising fundamental building blocks required for multi-container
application:

- **Services** key defines the compute aspects,
  implemented as one or more containers.

- **Networks** key defines how services communicate with
  each other.

- **Volumes** key defines how services store persistent data.

A sample reference Compose file is shown in Listing 7-1.

Listing 7-1. A Sample Docker Compose File

```
services:
    database:
      image: mysql
      environment:
        MYSQL_ROOT_PASSWORD: dontusethisinprod
      volumes:
        - db-data:/var/lib/mysql
    webserver:
      image: 'nginx:alpine'
      ports:
        - 8080:80
      depends_on:
        - cache
        - database
    cache:
      image: redis

volumes:
    db-data:
```

Similar to the Dockerfile, the Compose file is very readable and makes it easy to follow along. This compose file is for a typical web application that includes a webserver, a database server, and a caching server. The Compose file declares that when Docker Compose runs, it will bring up three services—the webserver, the database server, and the caching server. The webserver depends on the database and the cache service, which means that unless the database and the cache service are brought up, the webservice will not be brought up. The cache and the database keys indicate that for cache, Docker must bring up the Redis image and the MySQL image for the database.

To bring up all the containers, issue the following command:

```
docker-compose up -d
[+] Running 4/4
 :: Network code_default        Created   0.1s
 :: Container code_database_1    Started   1.2s
 :: Container code_cache_1       Started   1.1s
 :: Container code_webserver_1  Started   2.3s
```

Once the command is issued, Docker will bring up all the services in the background. Note that even though the Compose file has the definition of the database first, the webserver second, and the cache as the last, Docker still brings up the caching container and the database container before bringing up the webserver container. This is because you defined the depends_on key for the webserver as follows:

```
depends_on:
    - cache
    - database
```

This tells Docker to bring up the cache and the database containers first before bringing up the webserver. Docker Compose, however, will not wait and check that the cache container is ready to accept connections and then bring up the database container—it merely brings up the containers in the specified order.

You can see the logs by typing the following command:

```
docker-compose logs
```

```
webserver_1 | [notice] 1#1: nginx/1.21.1
database_1  | [Note] [Entrypoint]: Switching to dedicated user
'mysql'
cache_1     | # Server initialized
cache_1     | * Ready to accept connections
```

Docker will aggregate the STDOUT of each container and will be streaming them when run in the foreground. By default, docker-compose logs will only show a snapshot of the logs. If you want the logs to be streamed continuously, you can append the -f or --follow flag to tell Docker to keep streaming the logs. Alternatively, if you want to see the last *n* logs from each container, you can type this:

```
docker-compose logs --tail=n
```

where *n* is the required number of lines that you want to see. Stopping the containers is as simple as issuing the stop command, as shown here:

```
docker-compose stop

[+] Running 3/3
 :: Container code_webserver_1  Stopped    0.5s
 :: Container code_database_1   Stopped    1.4s
 :: Container code_cache_1      Stopped    0.4s
```

To resume the stopped containers, issue the start command:

```
docker-compose start
[+] Running 3/3
 :: Container code_database_1   Started  1.8s
 :: Container code_cache_1      Started  1.9s
 :: Container code_webserver_1  Started  0.7s
```

To completely tear down the containers, issue the following command:

```
docker-compose down
```

This will stop all containers and will also remove the associated containers, networks, and volumes that were created when docker-compose up was issued.

```
[+] Running 4/4
 ⠿ Container code_webserver_1   Removed   0.5s
 ⠿ Container code_cache_1       Removed   0.6s
 ⠿ Container code_database_1    Removed   1.3s
 ⠿ Network code_default         Removed   0.2s
```

Docker Compose File Reference

Recall that the Compose file is a YAML file for configuration that Docker reads and sets up the Compose job. This section explains what the different keys in a Docker Compose file do.

Services Key

Services is the first root key of the Compose YAML and it's the configuration of the container that needs to be created.

Build Key

The build key contains the configuration options that are applied at build time. The build key can be a path to the build context or a detailed object consisting of the context and optional Dockerfile location:

```
services:
    app:
        build: ./app

services:
    app:
        build:
            context: ./app
            Dockerfile: dockerfile-app
```

Context Key

The context key sets the context of the build. If the context is a relative
path, the path is considered relative to the Compose file's location.

```
build:
    context: ./app
    Dockerfile: dockerfile-app
```

Image Key

If the image tag is supplied along with the build option, Docker will build
the image, and then name and tag the image with the supplied image
name and tag.

```
services:
    app:
        build: ./app
        image: sathyabhat:app
```

environment/env_file Key

The environment key sets the environment variables for the application,
while env_file provides the path to the environment file that's read to set
the environment variables. Both environment and env_file can accept a
single file or multiple files as an array.

In the following example, for the app service, two environment
variables—PATH and API_KEY, with values /home and thisisnotavalidkey,
respectively—are set to the app service.

```
services:
    app:
        image: mysql
```

```
environment:
    PATH: /home
    API_KEY: thisisnotavalidkey
```

In the following example, the environment variables from a file called .env are fetched, and the values are assigned to the app service.

```
services:
  app:
      image: mysql
      env_file: .env
```

In the following example, multiple environment files defined under the env_file key are fetched, and the values are assigned to the app service.

```
services:
  app:
      image: mysql
      env_file:
          - common.env
          - app.env
          - secrets.env
```

depends_on Key

This key is used to set the dependency requirements across various services. Consider this config:

```
services:
    database:
        image: mysql
    webserver:
        image: nginx:alpine
```

```
    depends_on:
         - cache
         - database
  cache:
      image: redis
```

When `docker-compose` up is issued, Docker will bring up the services as per the defined dependency order. In the previous case, Docker brings up the cache and database services before bringing up the webserver service.

Caution   With the depends_on key, Docker will only bring up the services in the defined order; it will not wait for each service to be ready and then bring up the successive service.

Image Key

This key specifies the name of the image to be used when a container is brought up. If the image doesn't exist locally, Docker will attempt to pull it if the build key is not present. If the build key is in the Compose file, Docker will attempt to build and tag the image.

```
services:
    database:
        image: mysql
```

ports Key

This key specifies the ports that will be exposed to the port. When providing this key, you can specify both ports (i.e., the Docker host port to which the container port will be exposed or just the container port), in which case, a random, ephemeral port number on the host is selected.

```
services:
    database:
        image: nginx
        ports:
            - "8080:80"

services:
    database:
        image: nginx
        ports:
            - "80"
```

Volumes Key

Volumes is available as a top-level key as well as a suboption available to a service. When volumes are referred to as top-level keys, it lets you provide the named volumes that will be used for services at the bottom. The configuration for this looks like this:

```
services:
    database:
        image: mysql
        environment:
            MYSQL_ROOT_PASSWORD: dontusethisinprod
        volumes:
            - "dbdata:/var/lib/mysql"
    webserver:
        image: nginx:alpine
        depends_on:
            - cache
            - database
```

```
cache:
    image: redis

volumes:
  dbdata:
```

In the absence of the top-level volumes key, Docker will throw an error when creating the container. Consider the following configuration, where the volumes key has been skipped:

```
services:
  database:
    image: mysql
    environment:
      MYSQL_ROOT_PASSWORD: dontusethisinprod
    volumes:
        - "dbdata:/var/lib/mysql"
  webserver:
    image: nginx:alpine
    depends_on:
        - cache
        - database
  cache:
    image: redis
```

Trying to bring up the containers throws an error, as shown here:

```
docker-compose up
service "database" refers to undefined volume dbdata: invalid
compose project
```

It is possible to use bind mounts as well. Instead of referring to the named volume, all you have to do is provide the path. Consider this configuration:

```
services:
    database:
        image: mysql
        environment:
            MYSQL_ROOT_PASSWORD: dontusethisinprod
        volumes:
            - ./dbdir:/var/lib/mysql
    webserver:
        image: nginx:alpine
        depends_on:
            - cache
            - database
    cache:
        image:redis
```

The `volume` key has a value of `./dbdir:/var/lib/mysql`, which means Docker will mount `dbdir` in the current directory to the `/var/lib/mysql` directory of the container. Relative paths are considered in relation to the directory of the Compose file.

Restart Key

The restart key provides the restart policy for the container. By default, the restart policy is set as `no`, which means Docker will not restart the container, no matter what. The following restart policies are available:

- `no`: Container will never restart

- `always`: Container will always restart after exit

- `on-failure`: Container will restart if it exits due to an error

- `unless-stopped`: Container will always restart unless exited explicitly or if the Docker daemon is stopped

Docker Compose CLI Reference

The `docker-compose` command comes with its own set of subcommands. The following sections explain them.

The build Subcommand

The `build` command reads the Compose file, scans for build keys, and then proceeds to build and tag the image. The images are tagged as `project_service`. If the Compose file doesn't have a build key, Docker will skip building any images. The usage is as follows:

```
docker-compose build <options> <service...>
```

If the service name is provided, Docker will proceed to build the image for just that service. Otherwise, it will build images for all the services. Some of the commonly used options are as follows:

```
--compress: Compresses the build context
--no-cache Ignore the build cache when building the image
```

The down Subcommand

The down command stops the containers and will proceed to remove the containers, volumes, and networks. Its usage is as follows:

```
docker-compose down
```

The exec Subcommand

The `compose exec` command is equivalent to the `docker exec` command. It lets you run ad hoc commands on any of the containers. Its usage is as follows:

```
docker-compose exec  <service> <command>
```

The logs Subcommand

The logs command displays the log output from all the services. Its usage is as follows:

```
docker-compose logs <options> <service>
```

By default, logs will only show the last logs and for all services. You can show logs for just one service by providing the service name. The -f option follows the log output.

The stop subcommand

The stop command stops the containers. Its usage is as follows:

```
docker-compose stop
```

Exercises

BUILDING AND RUNNING A MYSQL DATABASE CONTAINER WITH A WEB UI FOR MANAGING THE DATABASE

In this exercise, you will build a multi-container application consisting of a container for the MySQL database and another container for adminer, a popular Web UI for MySQL. Since you already have prebuilt images for MySQL and adminer, you won't need to build them.

Tip   The source code, Dockerfile, and docker-compose files associated with this exercise are available on the GitHub repo of this book at https://github.com/Apress/practical-docker-with-python, in the source-code/chapter-7/exercise-1 directory.

You can start with the Docker Compose file, as follows:

```
services:
  mysql:
    image: mysql
    environment:
        MYSQL_ROOT_PASSWORD: dontusethisinprod
    ports:
        - 3306:3306
    volumes:
        - dbdata:/var/lib/mysql
  adminer:
    image: adminer
    ports:
        - 8080:8080

volumes:
    dbdata:
```

This Compose file combines everything that you learned in this book into one concise file. Since you are targeting the Compose spec, you can omit the version tag. Under Services, define two services—one for the database, which pulls in a Docker image called mysql. When the container is created, an environment variable, MYSQL_ROOT_PASSWORD, sets the root password for the database and port 3306 from the container is published to the host.

The data in the MySQL database is stored in a volume known as dbdata and is mounted to the /var/lib/mysql directory of the container. This is where MySQL stores the data. In other words, any data saved to the database in the container is handled by the volume named dbdata. The other service, called as adminer, just pulls in a Docker image called adminer and publishes port 8080 from the container to the host.

Validate the Compose file by typing the following command:

```
docker-compose config
```

If everything is okay, Docker will print out the Compose file as it as parsed; it should look like this:

```
services:
  adminer:
    image: adminer
    networks:
      default: null
    ports:
    - mode: ingress
      target: 8080
      published: 8080
      protocol: tcp
  mysql:
    environment:
      MYSQL_ROOT_PASSWORD: dontusethisinprod
    image: mysql
    networks:
      default: null
    ports:
    - mode: ingress
      target: 3306
      published: 3306
      protocol: tcp
    volumes:
    - type: volume
      source: dbdata
      target: /var/lib/mysql
      volume: {}
```

```
networks:
  default:
    name: docker-compose-adminer_default
volumes:
  dbdata:
```

Run all containers by typing the command as follows:

```
docker-compose up -d
```

The containers will start in the background, as shown here:

```
docker-compose up -d
[+] Running 3/3
 ⠿ Network docker-compose-adminer_default    Created   0.1s
 ⠿ Container docker-compose-adminer_adminer_1 Started   1.0s
 ⠿ Container docker-compose-adminer_mysql_1   Started   1.1s
```

Now take a look at the logs. Type the following command:

```
docker-compose logs
adminer_1  | PHP 7.4.22 Development Server (http://[::]:8080)
started
mysql_1    | [Note] [Entrypoint]: Entrypoint script for MySQL
Server 8.0.26-1debian10 started.
mysql_1    | [System] [MY-010931] [Server] /usr/sbin/mysqld:
ready for connections. Version: '8.0.26'
```

This tells you that the adminer UI and MySQL database are ready. Try logging in by navigating to http://localhost:8080. The adminer login page (see Figure 7-1) should load.

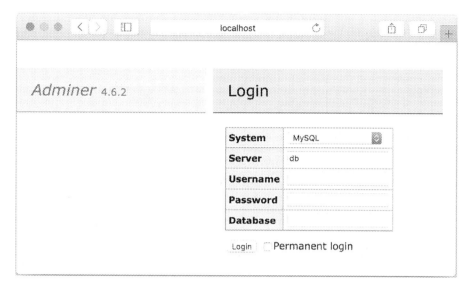

Figure 7-1. *adminer login page*

Notice that the server has been populated with the value db. Since docker-compose creates its own network for the application, the hostname for each container is the service name. In this case, the MySQL database service name is mysql and the database will be accessible via the mysql hostname. Enter the username as root and the password as the one entered in the MYSQL_ROOT_PASSWORD environment variable (see Figure 7-2).

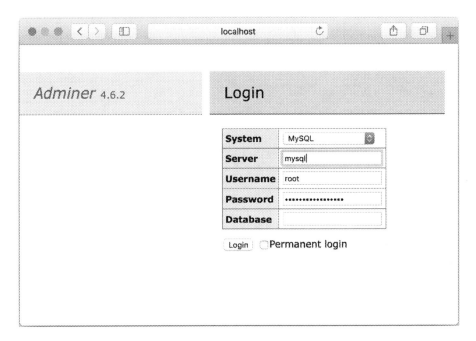

Figure 7-2. *adminer login details*

If the details are correct, you should see the database page shown in Figure 7-3.

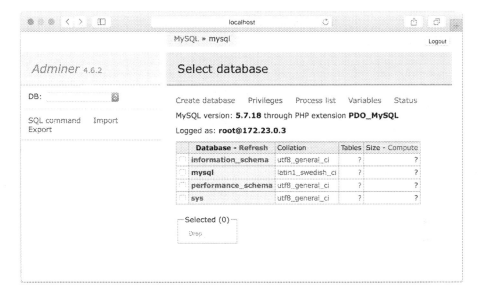

Figure 7-3. *Database details available once you're logged in*

CONVERTING NEWSBOT TO A DOCKER COMPOSE PROJECT

In the exercise in Chapter 6, you added volumes to Newsbot and the data was persisted to a MySQL container. You also brought up the newsbot and mysql containers separately and connected them to the common bridge network. In this exercise, you will write a Docker Compose file containing the Newsbot container and MySQL container, with an attached volume to persist the data. In this exercise, you will see how easy Docker Compose makes it to bring up multiple containers, each with their associated properties.

Tip   The source code, Dockerfile, and docker-compose files associated with this exercise are available on the GitHub repo of this book at https://github.com/Apress/practical-docker-with-python, in the source-code/chapter-7/exercise-2 directory.

Let's create a new Docker Compose file and add the following contents:

```
services:
  newsbot:
    build: .
    depends_on:
      - mysql
    restart: "on-failure"
    environment:
      - NBT_ACCESS_TOKEN=${NBT_ACCESS_TOKEN}
    networks:
      - newsbot

  mysql:
    image: mysql
    volumes:
        - newsbot-db:/var/lib/mysql
    environment:
        - MYSQL_ROOT_PASSWORD=dontusethisinprod
    networks:
      - newsbot

volumes:
  newsbot-db:

networks:
  newsbot:
```

Since you need two services, one for Newsbot and one for the MySQL server, there are keys corresponding to each of them. For Newsbot, you add a depends_on key with a value of mysql to indicate that the MySQL container should be started before Newsbot. But as you saw earlier, Docker doesn't wait for the MySQL container to be ready, so Newsbot has been modified to wait 60 seconds before attempting to connect to the mysql container. There is also a restart policy to restart the newsbot container on failure of the application.

Newsbot requires the Telegram bot API token, which you pass to the container environment variable NBT_ACCESS_TOKEN from the same host environment variable. Each of the two services also has a network key indicating that the containers are to be connected to the newsbot network. Finally, you add the top-level keys for volume and network, declared as newsbot-db for persisting MySQL data for the volume and newsbot as the network. You can verify that the Compose file is correct and valid by typing the config command shown here:

```
docker-compose config
```

Docker prints the config of the Compose that you wrote, similar to the Compose file itself.

```
services:
  mysql:
    environment:
      MYSQL_ROOT_PASSWORD: dontusethisinprod
    image: mysql
    networks:
      newsbot: null
    volumes:
    - type: volume
      source: newsbot-db
      target: /var/lib/mysql
      volume: {}
  newsbot:
    build:
      context: exercise-2/newsbot-compose
      dockerfile: exercise-2/newsbot-compose/Dockerfile
    depends_on:
      mysql:
        condition: service_started
    environment:
```

```
      NBT_ACCESS_TOKEN: ""
    networks:
      newsbot: null
    restart: on-failure
networks:
  newsbot:
    name: newsbot-compose_newsbot
volumes:
  newsbot-db:
    name: newsbot-compose_newsbot-db
```

Now run the Compose application. Don't forget to pass the <token> with the
value of the Newsbot API key that you generated in Chapter 3.

```
NBT_ACCESS_TOKEN=<token> docker-compose up
```

You should see the containers being built and started up, like this:

```
[+] Running 4/4
 ⠿ Network newsbot-compose_newsbot        Created    0.0s
 ⠿ Volume "newsbot-compose_newsbot-db"    Created    0.0s
 ⠿ Container newsbot-compose_mysql_1      Started    1.6s
 ⠿ Container newsbot-compose_newsbot_1    Started    1.8s

Attaching to mysql_1, newsbot_1
newsbot_1  | INFO:   <module> - Starting up
newsbot_1  | INFO:   <module> - Waiting for 60 seconds for db to
come up
mysql_1    | [System] [MY-013577] [InnoDB] InnoDB
initialization has ended.
mysql_1    | [System] [MY-010931] [Server] /usr/sbin/mysqld:
ready for connections. Version: '8.0.26'  socket: '/var/run/
mysqld/mysqld.sock'  port: 3306  MySQL Community Server - GPL.
newsbot_1  | INFO:   <module> - Checking on dbs
newsbot_1  | INFO:   get_updates - received response: {'ok':
True, 'result': []}
```

```
newsbot_1  | INFO:  get_updates - received response: {'ok':
True, 'result': []}
newsbot_1  | INFO:  get_updates - received response: {'ok':
True, 'result': []}
newsbot_1  | INFO:  get_updates - received response: {'ok':
True, 'result': []}
```

The last line indicates that the bot is working. Try setting a source and fetching the data by typing /sources docker and then /fetch into the Telegram bot. If all goes well, you should see the result in Figure 7-4.

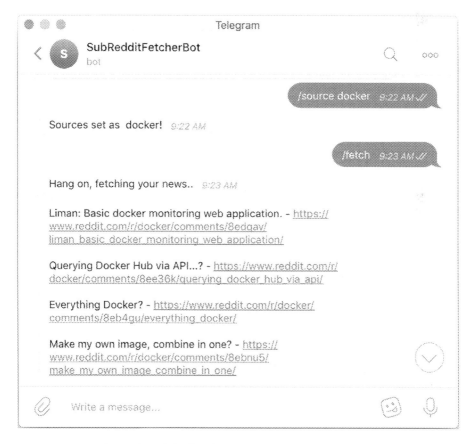

Figure 7-4. *The subreddit fetcher bot in action*

You can go one step further by modifying the Compose file to include the `adminer` service so that you have a WebUI to check that the contents are being saved to the database. Modify the existing Docker compose file to include the `adminer` service as shown here and save it to a file called `docker-compose.adminer.yml`:

```yaml
services:
  newsbot:
    build: .
    depends_on:
      - mysql
    restart: "on-failure"
    environment:
      - NBT_ACCESS_TOKEN=${NBT_ACCESS_TOKEN}
    networks:
      - newsbot

  mysql:
    image: mysql
    volumes:
        - newsbot-db:/var/lib/mysql
    environment:
        - MYSQL_ROOT_PASSWORD=dontusethisinprod
    networks:
      - newsbot

  adminer:
    image: adminer
    ports:
        - 8080:8080
    networks:
      - newsbot

  volumes:
    newsbot-db:
```

```
networks:
  newsbot:
```

Confirm that the Compose file is valid by typing the `config` command as follows:

```
docker-compose -f docker-compose.adminer.yml config
services:
  adminer:
    image: adminer
    networks:
      newsbot: null
    ports:
    - mode: ingress
      target: 8080
      published: 8080
      protocol: tcp
  mysql:
    environment:
      MYSQL_ROOT_PASSWORD: dontusethisinprod
    image: mysql
    networks:
      newsbot: null
    volumes:
    - type: volume
      source: newsbot-db
      target: /var/lib/mysql
      volume: {}
  newsbot:
    build:
      context: exercise-2/newsbot-compose
      dockerfile: exercise-2/newsbot-compose/Dockerfile
    depends_on:
      mysql:
        condition: service_started
```

```
    environment:
      NBT_ACCESS_TOKEN: ""
    networks:
      newsbot: null
    restart: on-failure
networks:
  newsbot:
    name: newsbot-compose_newsbot
volumes:
  newsbot-db:
    name: newsbot-compose_newsbot-db
```

Now tear down the existing Compose file using the following command:

```
docker-compose down
```

```
[+] Running 3/3
 ⣿ Container newsbot-compose_newsbot_1   Removed        1.0s
 ⣿ Container newsbot-compose_mysql_1     Removed        0.1s
 ⣿ Network newsbot-compose_newsbot       Removed        0.1s
```

Since the data is persisted to volumes, you shouldn't be worried about data loss.

Bring up the service again using the following command. Don't forget to pass the <token> with the value of the Newsbot API key that you generated in Chapter 3.

```
NBT_ACCESS_TOKEN=<token> docker-compose -f docker-compose.
adminer.yml up
```

```
Running 4/4
 ⣿ Network newsbot-compose_newsbot        Created  0.1s
 ⣿ Container newsbot-compose_adminer_1    Started  7.1s
 ⣿ Container newsbot-compose_mysql_1      Started  7.1s
 ⣿ Container newsbot-compose_newsbot_1    Started  5.1s
Attaching to adminer_1, mysql_1, newsbot_1
```

```
mysql_1    | [System] [MY-010931] [Server] /usr/sbin/mysqld:
ready for connections. Version: '8.0.26'  socket: '/var/run/
mysqld/mysqld.sock'  port: 3306  MySQL Community Server - GPL.
newsbot_1  | INFO: <module> - Starting up
newsbot_1  | INFO: <module> - Waiting for 60 seconds for db to
come up
newsbot_1  | INFO: <module> - Checking on dbs
newsbot_1  | INFO: get_updates - received response: {'ok': True,
'result': []}
```

Navigate to adminer by heading to http://localhost:8080. Log in using
the root username, with the password set in the MYSQL_ROOT_PASSWORD
value and the Server value as mysql. Click the Newsbot database, source as
the table, and then choose Select Data. You should see the subreddit that you
earlier set to source (see Figure 7-5).

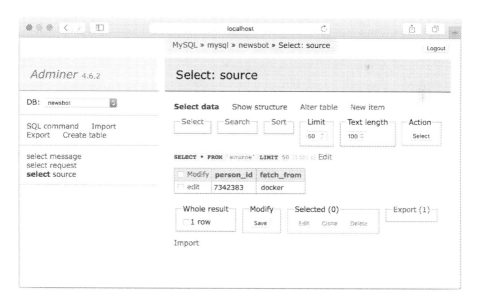

Figure 7-5. *The project running with data saved to the database*

Success! The application is running, and the data is saved to the MySQL
database and persisted, despite removing and re-creating the containers.

197

Summary

In this chapter, you learned about Docker Compose, including how to install it and why it is used. You also took a deep dive into the Docker Compose file and the CLI. You ran some exercises on building multi-containers applications with Docker Compose. You also learned how to extend the Newsbot project to a multi-container application using Docker Compose, by adding a linked database and a Web UI to edit the database.

CHAPTER 8

Preparing for Production Deployments

In the previous chapters, you learned about Docker and its associated terminologies and took a deeper look into how to build Docker images using the Dockerfile. You also learned how to persist data generated by containers and you enabled network communication across the running containers with help of Docker's network features. You then learned how Docker Compose makes it easy to run multi-container applications by writing your requirements in a simple YAML file and providing that as an input to Docker Compose.

In this chapter, you learn how to prepare your Docker image to deploy your application in production, including a brief overview of Continuous Integration, and how to set up Continuous Integration with GitHub Actions. The chapter touches upon container orchestration and the various orchestrators available. It includes an overview of one of the most popular container orchestrators in the market, Kubernetes.

© Sathyajith Bhat 2022
S. Bhat, *Practical Docker with Python*, https://doi.org/10.1007/978-1-4842-7815-4_8

Continuous Integration (CI)

Continuous Integration is the practice of automatically having each developer's code changes merged into the main branch of a source code repository, multiple times a day. Along with merge, the process also runs different tests—including unit tests, integration tests, functional tests—and when all the tests pass, a build artifact is created and saved, usually to some sort of artifact storage.

This generated artifact is taken into the next steps, deployed to development and staging environments to form what is known as the CI/CD (Continuous Integration/Continuous Delivery) pipeline. As the software build and test process matures, it is not uncommon for many teams to switch from Continuous Delivery to Continuous Deployment. In Continuous Delivery, the final artifact is ready to be deployed at any time, but the deployment is usually manually initiated. Continuous Deployment completely automates the end-to-end build-to-release pipeline, with the final build artifacts being automatically deployed as well.

CI/CD has become quite popular in today's software development lifecycle because of the rapid feedback cycle a CI/CD pipeline provides. With a well-defined pipeline, it's possible for a developer to open a GitHub Pull Request with the changes to their source, have the Continuous Integration pipeline kick into effect, start the tests for the new code, get a static analysis done, and have an artifact ready for deployment, all in a span of a few minutes, and automatically with no one having to start anything or run things manually.

With Docker, CI/CD becomes even more effortless. With Dockerfile, there's a simple, reproducible way to rebuild the required image with the dependencies, and the Docker image's portability means that the image can run on any host that has the Docker daemon installed on it. This is an important distinction from the previous way of packaged software. The Docker image is self-contained. No more hassles about getting the dependencies right with the required versions, host OS dependencies, and so on. For microservices, testing dependent systems as part of source code check-in becomes even easier. With a Docker Compose file that has the required services defined, a simple `docker-compose up` is sufficient to bring up the services and test them.

There are many CI tools in the market, and most of the Source Code Management (SCM) systems—such as GitHub and GitLab—themselves provide a subset of Continuous Integration features. The next section explains how to set up Continuous Integration on GitHub using GitHub Actions.

GitHub Actions

GitHub Actions makes it easy to set up automated deploys and workflows that revolve around the Git repository you're working on. With GitHub Actions, you can define a workflow that gets triggered on every commit or push it to a branch to do a variety of actions. These actions can vary from simplistic echoes to complex linting, spinning up multiple containers.

GitHub Actions are event driven, so a workflow is triggered based on specific events such as a new pull request being opened or a new commit being pushed to the repository, just to name a few. Every event triggers a workflow. A workflow can have one or more jobs, and a job can include a series of steps to build, test, package, or release on GitHub or elsewhere, such as the Python Package Index (PyPI) or Docker Hub.

GitHub Actions run on servers called *runners*. Runners have the GitHub Actions runner application installed on them, listening for commands. GitHub provides hosted runners, but you can run your own runners. This is especially useful if you have compliance requirements to build the software in your own environment.

The steps to be performed as part of the pipeline are defined using a file known as the Actions Workflow file. The workflow file uses a YAML-based specification to define the events, jobs, and steps that need to be run, with support for conditionals to allow for specific jobs to run when conditions are met. For GitHub Actions to pick up and run a workflow, GitHub expects these workflow files to be saved in the `.github/workflows` directory at the root of the repository.

In this section, you will write a sample workflow file that will run on each commit. Before proceeding, you should have an empty public GitHub repo to test GitHub Actions. A sample workflow file is shown in Listing 8-1.

Listing 8-1. A Sample Github Actions Workflow File

```
name: Run compose
on: [push]

jobs:
  run-compose:
    timeout-minutes: 10
    runs-on: ubuntu-latest

    steps:
    - name: Checkout
      uses: actions/checkout@v1
    - name: Start containers
      run: docker-compose version
```

Tip   The syntax and the keys for the Actions spec file are available on the GitHub documentation page at `https://docs.github.com/en/actions/reference/workflow-syntax-for-github-actions`.

There are various keys in the Actions YAML file that you can examine:

- `name`: The `name` key defines the name of the workflow file that will be shown on the Actions tab.

- `on`: The `on` key defines the event during which the workflow will be triggered. This lets you determine at what point or during which event the workflow should be run.

- `timeout-minutes`: The `timeout` key lets you define how long a job can run before being cancelled by GitHub.

- `runs-on`: The `runs-on` key defines the runner on which the job runs.

- `steps`: The `steps` key defines the steps a specific job must run.

- `uses`: This key tells GitHub to fetch a specific action. Besides the steps you can run, GitHub Actions also allow you to use third-party actions that you have developed, reducing the need to rebuild everything. In this specific example, you instruct GitHub Actions to fetch the checkout action, which does a Git checkout and downloads the source code to the runner.

- `run`: The `run` key lets you define custom commands that can be run. This is useful when you want to run something that is not covered by the custom commands.

Looking at the Actions workflow file again, it defines a GitHub runner that will check out the source code and run a `docker-compose version` command.

Save this file as `.github/workflows/compose.yaml`, commit the files, and push this to the GitHub repo. Once you push the commit to the remote repository, GitHub should start the workflow immediately. From your GitHub repository page, click the Actions tab, and you can see the result of the workflow.

If you prefer a CLI approach, GitHub has a CLI tool that can give you feedback without having to open a tab and navigate to actions. To get started, you need to install the GitHub CLI, as mentioned in `https://cli.github.com/`.

Once the CLI is installed, open a new terminal session. Authenticate with GitHub by typing the following command:

```
gh auth login
```

Follow the instructions and you should be able to log in successfully. Once you're logged in, switch to the public repo directory that you created. Change to the newly cloned repo using the following command:

```
cd <repo>
```

Once in the repo, you can look at the workflows using the `gh workflow list` command:

```
gh workflow list
```

This should show only one workflow, the one that you created, as shown here:

```
gh workflow list
Run compose   active   <workflow id>
```

The number at the end is the ID of the workflow. You can examine the results of the workflow using the `workflow view` command, as shown here:

```
gh workflow view <workflow id>
```

```
Run compose - compose.yaml
ID: <workflow id>
```

```
Total runs 1
Recent runs
✓  test actions  Run compose  master  push  <run id>
```

You can dive deeper into this run by using the gh run command, as shown here:

```
gh run view <run id>
```

```
✓ master Run compose · <run id>
Triggered via push about 10 hours ago
```

```
JOBS
✓ run-compose in 5s (ID <job id>)
```

You can further dig into the results of the job with the job ID and the gh run command with the --job parameter:

```
gh run view --job <job id>
```

```
✓ master Run compose · <run id>
Triggered via push about 10 hours ago
```

```
✓ run-compose in 5s (ID <job id>)
  ✓ Set up job
  ✓ Checkout
  ✓ Start containers
  ✓ Complete job
```

Thus, with a simple YAML file, you've defined and set up your Continuous Integration workflow, which will get automatically triggered upon every new push. This example only shows a simple example of running a `docker-compose version` command. However, with the wealth of custom community-built actions as well as support for custom commands, it is easy to set up a comprehensive Continuous Integration system that can run linters, perform container security checks, and even build a new image. Later in the chapter, as part of the exercise, you will see this in action and set up a CI system for Newsbot so that a new Docker image gets built on every push.

Container Orchestration

Orchestration is the process of deploying a container to a suitable host (or many hosts) and managing the lifecycle of the deployed containers, including scaling up or down the number of containers as well as the underlying nodes based on the different metrics, such as CPU/memory utilization, network traffic, and so on. Orchestration also handles replacing the nodes and containers when they crash or error out. Orchestrators are used to perform many of the manual tasks that are needed to keep the containers running smoothly, without the need for manual intervention by human operators.

The Need for Orchestrators

Earlier, you learned that containers make it easy to deploy applications. With a single command, you can get one or more services up and running, with the required dependencies self-contained within the Docker image, or multiple linked containers that are expressed in Docker Compose files. The question then arises—if the application and dependencies are self-contained, why do you need orchestrators?

Containers ease the pain of running linked services for a developer. Developers can build their images, run them locally, and continue working on the local changes without having to update the local development setup or deploy the software to designated development environments. This process would be evolving and changing, especially when you have multiple people working on projects. By eliminating the toil involved in running software and empowering a developer to run their applications with a simple docker run or docker-compose up, Docker makes it easier to iterate and build.

In a production landscape, things get much more complicated. Containers make production deployments easier, but having to run many containers and having to maintain their lifecycle becomes a tedious affair. Why would you need to run multiple containers, you might wonder.

Consider Newsbot, the chatbot application that you've been working on throughout this book. It is a simple Python application that keeps polling the Telegram bot API, responds to messages, and posts back to Telegram. When you have a fewer number of requests, a single container is enough to respond to requests in a timely manner. However, as more people start using it, the number of requests the bot must handle increases significantly, and at a certain point, having just one container will be insufficient to respond to the requests. To cope with the demand, you need to scale up by increasing the number of containers. Without orchestrators, to do this, you have to run the command to bring up new containers. Doing this once or twice is okay, but having to do this repeatedly is not feasible. This is where orchestrators come in.

How Do Orchestrators Work?

While exact implementations of orchestrators differ across various tools, the general process remains the same. Most orchestrators are usually segmented into two tiers:

- Control tier, also known as the control plane
- Worker tier, also known as the worker plane

The control plane of an orchestrator handles incoming requests and operations related to controlling, running, and managing the orchestrator, while the worker plane handles the actual scheduling and orchestration of the containers in the designated nodes.

The orchestration process starts with a declarative description of the intended goal: this can be a YAML or a JSON file that describes what services to run, where to download the required container images (typically pointing to a Container registry), the number of replicas to run, what type of networking is needed to link the containers, and where to store the persistent data. If this looks like the Docker Compose file you learned about in Chapter 7, that is a valid observation.

A Compose Spec file describes these exact requirements. However, Docker Compose was meant and designed for single nodes. It cannot orchestrate a container across multiple nodes and is not suitable as an orchestrator, especially for workloads that span multiple nodes. For single-node workloads, however, it might be easier and simpler to use Docker Compose.

Once the orchestrator receives a request to increase the number of containers or to deploy a new container, it will perform a series of steps before running the container:

- The scheduler determines the node where the container is to be scheduled. This is done based on several constraints that may be in place, such as the required memory, CPU needed by the container, whether a GPU or specific classes of storage are required, and so on.

- A suitable node is selected; a request is sent to start the container. This includes different steps such as pulling the Docker image (if it is not present already), setting up the container network, and associating with the required volumes.

- Start the container.

- If the container has been configured with health checks, wait for the health checks to be positive before signaling that the container is ready to accept the workload.

- Once the container is up and running, the orchestrator will continuously monitor the health check of the container. If the health check fails, the orchestrator will terminate the container and bring up a new container in its place.

This entire process happens continuously in a loop and the orchestrator checks every few seconds for every container request that has been submitted to the orchestrator.

Popular Orchestrators

Kubernetes is quite possibly the most popular orchestrator but is no means the only orchestrator around. Other orchestrators that are available include:

- Docker Swarm

- DC/OS

- HashiCorp Nomad

With DC/OS reaching end-of-life and longer being supported, HashiCorp Nomad is slowly becoming more popular in smaller companies that do not need all the bells and whistles of Kubernetes. Another point to note is that you don't have to run a container orchestrator yourself to make the best use of containers. There are many managed container orchestrators that handle the control plane of the orchestrator. This frees you of the operational burden of having to run, maintain, and upgrade the control plane of the clusters and you can focus purely on running and maintaining your application. Some of these managed orchestrators include:

- Amazon EKS

- Amazon ECS

- Amazon Fargate

- Azure Kubernetes Service

- Azure Container Instances

- Google Kubernetes Engine

- Google Cloud Run

Amazon ECS, Amazon Fargate, Azure Container Instances, and Google Cloud Run use each company's respective proprietary orchestration engines and have their custom specifications that need to be submitted, after which the containers will be scheduled and orchestrated.

Amazon EKS, Azure Kubernetes Service, and Google Kubernetes Engine are managed Kubernetes services that support all the features that you expect from a Kubernetes provider. Kubernetes is a huge topic and covering all its features is a topic for another book and out of scope for this chapter. For this reason, the next sections bring up a test Kubernetes cluster using kind (Kubernetes in Docker) and attempt to run some sample applications.

Kubernetes

Kubernetes (also known as *k8s*) has emerged as the most popular container orchestrator today. Kubernetes is an open source system for deploying, scaling, operating, and managing containerized applications. Kubernetes was created by a group of Google engineers who used their experience running Borg, an internal container orchestrator at Google, to build an open source project. Kubernetes simplifies some complexities and eases the pain points observed while using Borg. Kubernetes gained popularity due to the relative ease of use and the features it provides out of the box, including but not limited to:

- Automated rollouts and rollbacks

- Full container lifecycle management

- Support for horizontal and vertical scaling

- Self-healing capabilities, including container and node-level failure resilience

- Advanced Role-Based Access Control (RBAC) features to allow access only to authorized users and groups

A Kubernetes cluster has various nodes that run containerized applications. These nodes are usually powered by virtual machines running in the cloud. In the industry, Kubernetes nodes are also seen running on powerful bare-metal hardware running in on-premises data center machines as well as at the edge, running on low-power devices. As noted in the previous section, the nodes are further segmented into Kubernetes control planes and worker planes, which include various components.

Kubernetes Control Plane

The Kubernetes control plane components control the state of the cluster and managing the workloads to be scheduled across the cluster. The control plane includes various components, and each component can be run on either a single master node or multiple master nodes, where high availability and fault tolerance is required. The control plane components include:

- **Kubernetes API server (or kube-apiserver)**: The kube-apiserver exposes the Kubernetes API and acts as a frontend to the cluster, through which any request to the Kubernetes cluster is accepted.

- **Etcd**: etcd is a highly available key-value store that is used as the backing store for Kubernetes cluster data. Losing etcd is a catastrophic loss and as such all measures should be taken to back up the data periodically.

- **Scheduler**: The Kubernetes Scheduler constantly monitors the available nodes onto which the workloads can be scheduled. When new requests come to start a new workload, it determines and schedules the relevant node where the workload can be scheduled.

- **Controller manager**: A controller is a process that is responsible for maintaining the status of individual subcomponents, such as the status of individual nodes, one-time jobs, among others. The controller manager runs each of these controllers and ensures that they are working as expected.

Kubernetes Worker Plane

The Kubernetes worker plane includes one or many worker nodes, with each node running various node components that maintain the workloads. The components include:

- **Kubelet**: The kubelet is a process that runs on every node in the cluster and registers the node it is running with the API server to accept workloads. The kubelet ensures that the containers and workloads are running in the node and maintains the lifecycle of a container, as directed by the API server.

- **Kube-proxy**: The kube-proxy is a network proxy that runs on every node and implements the networking features of Kubernetes. The kube-proxy maintains the network rules and sessions and routes traffic to the desired containers.

Most of the interactions with the Kubernetes are via the API, and the kubectl command-line application lets you control Kubernetes clusters by talking to the Kubernetes API. The kubectl application implements all the commands required to interact with the cluster and, internally, kubectl converts the API calls into respective API calls to the kube-apiserver to perform these actions.

A Look at kind

Setting up an entire Kubernetes cluster is quite an elaborate and tedious process that involves lots of steps, including creating and provisioning TLS certificates, provisioning the required nodes and installing the various components, joining the various worker and master nodes, and so on. While setting this up for a production use case can be done using various tools such as kOps (Kubernetes Operations), kubeadm, and so on, to test locally, you do not have to use these.

kind, short for Kubernetes in Docker, is a tool for running local Kubernetes clusters using Docker containers acting as nodes. The Kubernetes project itself uses kind to test cluster releases, and you can use kind for local development and testing. kind consists of a self-contained Go binary that interacts with Docker CLI to bring up and configure the Kubernetes clusters with almost no configuration for a single node cluster. If you need to simulate multiple nodes, you can provide a configuration file with the required number of nodes to bootstrap such a cluster.

Creating Kubernetes Clusters Using kind

Before you can create the Kubernetes clusters, you need to download and install kind. This can be done by heading over to kind's static releases page on GitHub at https://github.com/kubernetes-sigs/kind/releases. Once the required binary has been installed, you can invoke kind by providing the full path on the disk where kind is saved.

Note   This section refers only to the kind command, but be sure to substitute the full path to the kind binary, especially if the kind binary has not been moved to a location referenced by the PATH variable.

You also need to download and install kubectl, the command-line program that is used to interact with Kubernetes clusters. You can do this by following the instructions present in the Kubernetes documentation page at https://kubernetes.io/docs/tasks/tools/.

To create a cluster, run the following command:

```
kind create cluster --name kind
```

The cluster creation can take a couple of minutes, but once it is done, you should see these logs:

```
kind create cluster --name kind


Creating cluster "kind" ...
 ✓ Ensuring node image (kindest/node:v1.21.1) 🖼
 ✓ Preparing nodes 📦
 ✓ Writing configuration 📜
 ✓ Starting control-plane 🕹
 ✓ Installing CNI 🔌
```

✓ Installing StorageClass 💾
Set kubectl context to "kind-kind"
You can now use your cluster with:

kubectl cluster-info --context kind-kind

Thanks for using kind! 😊

You can look at the containers brought up by kind using the docker ps command, as shown here:

```
docker ps
CONTAINER ID    IMAGE                 NAMES
5a5ba27eac95    kindest/node:v1.21.1  kind-control-plane
```

Now look at the pods that are running in the cluster. To do this, type the following command:

```
kubectl get pods -A
```

This command lists all the running pods. A *pod* is the smallest execution unit in Kubernetes. By default, kubectl commands fetch resources from the namespace that is currently activated as a context. To show pods from all namespaces, including the system namespaces, pass the flag -A.

```
NAME                        READY   STATUS
coredns-6p84s               1/1     Running
coredns-ctpsm               1/1     Running
etcd                        1/1     Running
kindnet-76dht               1/1     Running
kube-apiserver              1/1     Running
kube-controller-manager     1/1     Running
kube-proxy-87lbc            1/1     Running
kube-scheduler              1/1     Running
```

From the running pods, you can see various pods, each corresponding to the component you learned about in the previous section. To delete the cluster, type the delete command, as shown here:

```
kind delete cluster --name kind
```

Running a Sample Service in Kubernetes

Now that you understand container orchestration a little better, let's see how you can take a Docker image and orchestrate it. For this section, you will create a sample Kubernetes cluster using kind. Once you have a cluster running, you will deploy a sample nginx container. While the Docker image is simplistic, it gives you a good idea of the steps needed when you go from running containers locally using a docker run command to deploying a container using Kubernetes.

First, you will create a new Kubernetes cluster using kind. Type the following command to start the cluster:

```
kind create cluster --name nginx-deploy
Creating cluster "nginx-deploy" ...
 ✓ Ensuring node image (kindest/node:v1.21.1) 🐳
 ✓ Preparing nodes 📦
 ✓ Writing configuration 📜
 ✓ Starting control-plane 🕹️
 ✓ Installing CNI 🔌
 ✓ Installing StorageClass 💾
Set kubectl context to "kind-nginx-deploy"
You can now use your cluster with:

kubectl cluster-info --context kind-nginx-deploy
Thanks for using kind! 😊
```

Pods and Deployments

In Kubernetes, a *pod* is the core component for running applications. A pod has at least one container but can also accommodate groups of related containers. A *deployment* is a Kubernetes object that creates pods, tells Kubernetes how many copies of pods should be created, and indicates when/how a new pod should be updated. To create a deployment, you can apply a YAML file with the Kubernetes specification that describes the pods to run.

Alternatively, for a quick start, you can also use the kubectl application to create a deployment, passing only the name of the Docker image with which the deployment is to be created. This is suitable for quick test deploys, but isn't recommended for full deploys. To create a deployment with a Docker image, run the command shown here:

```
kubectl create deployment nginx --image <docker image:tag>
```

To create a Kubernetes deployment with a Docker image, use this command:

```
kubectl create deployment nginx    --image nginx:1.21
deployment.apps/nginx created
```

While this command lets you create a sample deployment quickly, updating the existing deployment can get tedious. By creating a Kubernetes spec YAML and updating the YAML as and when you desire, you can instruct kubectl to apply the YAML file. Let's examine the spec of the deploy that was created because of this deployment. To do this, type the following command:

```
kubectl get deploy nginx -o yaml > nginx-deploy.yaml
```

This will output the deployment specification in a YAML format and save it to a file called nginx-deploy.yaml. Open this file in your favorite code editor. You should see the contents of the file, as shown in Listing 8-2.

Listing 8-2. A Kubernetes Deployment Object Specification File in YAML

```yaml
apiVersion: apps/v1
kind: Deployment
metadata:
  labels:
    app: nginx
  name: nginx
  namespace: default
spec:
  replicas: 1
  selector:
    matchLabels:
      app: nginx
  strategy:
    rollingUpdate:
      maxSurge: 25%
      maxUnavailable: 25%
    type: RollingUpdate
  template:
    metadata:
      creationTimestamp: null
      labels:
        app: nginx
    spec:
      containers:
      - image: nginx:1.21
        imagePullPolicy: IfNotPresent
        name: nginx
        resources: {}
```

```
      terminationMessagePath: /dev/termination-log
      terminationMessagePolicy: File
    restartPolicy: Always
    schedulerName: default-scheduler
    securityContext: {}
    terminationGracePeriodSeconds: 30
status: {}
```

While an in-depth explanation of each of these fields would be out of scope for this book, it is still worth noting several additional features that an orchestrator like Kubernetes can provide over a container being started and run using the docker run command. Some of the noteworthy features include:

- A *namespace* key to isolate applications in their own scope, allowing for stronger application of role-based access policies.

- *Labels* to allow objects to be identified across the cluster.

- A *replicas* key, indicating how many replicas of the container the orchestrator should always maintain.

- A *strategy* object to indicate how a new container image should be deployed, how many new containers should be rolled out, and what the tolerance percent should be for the number of unavailable containers.

- An *imagePullPolicy* that describes when and how the container images are to be pulled from the container registry.

These are just some features for a Deployment object. Kubernetes supports more built-in objects for specialized workloads:

- A *StatefulSet* lets you run one or many pods for which the persistence and state need to be tracked (for example, database workloads).

- A *DaemonSet* runs the pods on every node of the cluster (for example, logging agents).

- Jobs and CronJobs run one-off tasks and stop when they're done.

Thus, orchestrators provide a world of features for running various and specialized workloads. Not everyone who needs containers will benefit from orchestrators, because of the overhead involved in running and maintaining them. For a large organization, an orchestrator is an invaluable investment when considering moving the workloads to containers.

Exercises

In this chapter, you learned about basic Continuous Integration and Container Orchestration. Now you can try some hands-on exercises on building a Continuous Integration workflow and running a multi-node orchestrator using kind and Kubernetes on a local computer.

CREATING MULTI-NODE CLUSTERS WITH KIND

You learned earlier that kind, short for Kubernetes in Docker, is a tool for running local Kubernetes clusters using Docker containers acting as nodes. For this exercise, you will learn how you can spin up a multi-node Kubernetes cluster using kind.

Tip   The kind configuration file associated with this exercise is available on the GitHub repo of this book at https://github.com/ Apress/practical-docker-with-python, in the source-code/chapter-8/exercise-1 directory.

---

kind makes it easy to create multi-node clusters to test locally. For this, first create a kind configuration file in YAML. The config file in Listing 8-3 shows the configuration that is needed to create a multi-node cluster with three control-plane nodes and three workers.

Listing 8-3. Configuration Needed to Create a Multi-Node Cluster

```
kind: Cluster
apiVersion: kind.x-k8s.io/v1alpha4
nodes:
- role: control-plane
- role: control-plane
- role: control-plane
- role: worker
- role: worker
- role: worker
```

Save the file as `kind-multi-node.yml`. Now, create a new cluster using the command you used before, but with an extra flag (to use this file as the configuration file), as shown here:

```
kind create cluster --name kind-multi-node --config kind-multi-
node.yml
```

The cluster creation can take a couple of minutes, but once it is done, you should see the logs shown here:

```
Creating cluster "kind-multi-node" ...
 ✓ Ensuring node image (kindest/node:v1.21.1) 🖼
 ✓ Preparing nodes 📦 📦 📦 📦 📦 📦
 ✓ Configuring the external load balancer ⚖
 ✓ Writing configuration 📜
 ✓ Starting control-plane 🕹
 ✓ Installing CNI 🔌
 ✓ Installing StorageClass 💾
 ✓ Joining more control-plane nodes 🎮
 ✓ Joining worker nodes 🚜
Set kubectl context to "kind-kind-multi-node"
You can now use your cluster with:

kubectl cluster-info --context kind-kind-multi-node
Not sure what to do next? 😅  Check out https://kind.sigs.k8s.
io/docs/user/quick-start/
```

You can look at the containers brought up by `kind` by using the `docker ps` command, as shown here:

```
CONTAINER ID    IMAGE                   NAMES
0f27d1316302    kindest/haproxy:v202    kind-multi-node-external-
                                        load-balancer

2a5b37dc51cc    kindest/node:v1.21.1    kind-multi-node-worker
4413cc424783    kindest/node:v1.21.1    kind-multi-node-control-
                                        plane2
```

bf6f2db610d9	kindest/node:v1.21.1	kind-multi-node-control-plane3
c11c07e67abd	kindest/node:v1.21.1	kind-multi-node-worker3
02afa01cdce6	kindest/node:v1.21.1	kind-multi-node-control-plane
e2e2d427a70f	kindest/node:v1.21.1	kind-multi-node-worker2

Since kind uses a container as a way to simulate nodes, you can see that there are three control-plane nodes, three worker nodes, and an external load balancer node to route the traffic coming into the cluster. With a multi-node Kubernetes cluster available at your disposal, running your containerized applications on a production-grade orchestrator is easy.

SETTING UP CONTINUOUS INTEGRATION FOR NEWSBOT

In this exercise, you will set up a Continuous Integration workflow for Newsbot that will run *flake8*, build the Docker image, and push the resulting image to Docker Hub. The Continuous Integration workflow will be set up using GitHub Actions, but the same principle could be applied using any Continuous Integration tool.

Tip   The source code and Dockerfile associated with this exercise, as well as the GitHub Actions workflow file, are all available on the GitHub repo of this book at https://github.com/Apress/practical-docker-with-python, in the source-code/chapter-8/exercise-2 directory.

This exercise also assumes that you are working with the Newsbot source code and the Dockerfile from Chapter 7, Exercise 2. You will also be setting up the workflow for the repo of the book, that is, https://github.com/ Apress/practical-docker-with-python. You are encouraged to fork this repo, clone it to your local computer, and practice this in your fork or implement the same in a completely different repository.

Earlier in the chapter, you learned that the GitHub Actions workflow file is a YAML-based spec file. Let's start with the sample spec file that you used earlier. You will modify this to add three steps:

1. Check out the source code.

2. Install the required Python version.

3. Install the required dependencies using pip.

The workflow file is shown in Listing 8-4.

Listing 8-4. GitHub Actions Workflow File to Install the Dependencies

```
name: Lint and build Docker
on: [push, pull_request]

jobs:
  lint:
    timeout-minutes: 10
    runs-on: ubuntu-latest

    steps:
    - name: Checkout
      uses: actions/checkout@v1

    - name: Setup Python
      uses: actions/setup-python@v2
      with:
        python-version: "3.7"
```

```
- name: Install Dependencies
  run: |
    python -m pip install --upgrade pip
    pwd
    cd source-code/chapter-7/exercise-2/newsbot-compose
    pip install -r requirements.txt
```

Save this file to .github/workflows/build-newsbot.yaml in the Git repository, commit the changes, and push the changes to GitHub. The GitHub Action should trigger immediately. As you saw earlier, you'll use the GitHub CLI to verify that the action was triggered.

First verify that the workflow was created. Type the following command:

```
gh workflow list
```

Remember to select the correct base repository if prompted. You should see a result like this one:

```
gh workflow list
Lint and build Docker  active  <workflow id>
```

You can examine a summary of the workflow status using the following command:

```
gh workflow view <workflow id>
Lint and build Docker - build-newsbot.yaml
ID: <workflow id>

Total runs 1
Recent runs
✓  add workflow  Lint and build Docker  add-lint-build-
workflow  push  <run id>
```

The tick indicates that the workflow run was successful. You can examine the details of the run in further detail, as you learned earlier, but for now, it's sufficient to know it was successful. Let's add some more steps to the workflow.

Most CI workflows will have some sort of Linting and Style Guide reporter so that the written code adheres to the programming languages and/or the organization's guidelines. For this workflow, you will add flake8, which will analyze the code and provide suggestions for improvements. With this change, the GitHub Actions workflow file now looks like Listing 8-5.

Listing 8-5. GitHub Actions Workflow Updated to Analyze Source Code

```
name: Lint and build Docker
on: [push, pull_request]

jobs:
  lint:
    timeout-minutes: 10
    runs-on: ubuntu-latest

    steps:
    - name: Checkout
      uses: actions/checkout@v1

    - name: Setup Python
      uses: actions/setup-python@v2
      with:
        python-version: "3.7"

    - name: Install Dependencies
      run: |
        python -m pip install --upgrade pip
        cd source-code/chapter-7/exercise-2/newsbot-compose
        pip install -r requirements.txt

    - name: Lint with flake8
      run: |
        pip install flake8
        cd source-code/chapter-7/exercise-2/newsbot-compose
```

```
# run flake8 first to detect any python syntax errors
flake8 . --count --select=E9,F63,F7,F82 --show-source
--statistics
# run again to exit treating all errors as warnings
flake8 . --count --exit-zero --max-complexity=10
--statistics
```

Save the changes, commit them to the repo, and push the changes to the remote. This should trigger the workflow run again, and you can examine the run using the gh CLI app. Since you know that the workflow exists, you can look at the most recent workflow runs instead, using the following command:

```
gh run list
STATUS  NAME                 WORKFLOW              ID
✓       <commit message>  Lint and build Docker  <run id>
X       <commit message>  Lint and build Docker  <run id>
✓       <commit message>  Lint and build Docker  <run id>
```

You're interested in the details of the last run, so look at it using the following command, taking care to substitute the value of run ID from the output of the previous command:

```
gh run view <run id>
```

You should get a result similar to this one shown here:

```
gh run view <run id>
✓ add-lint-build-workflow Lint and build Docker · <run id>
Triggered via push about 4 minutes ago
JOBS
✓ lint in 17s (ID <job id>)
```

Thus, the Lint is working as expected. Let's extend this workflow to add a Docker Build and Push job. You define a new job, called docker-build, and the steps to check out the code and run the docker build command.

Since this runs on every pull request or pushes, instead of tagging it with an arbitrary version, you can use GITHUB_SHA, which is an environment variable exposed by GitHub that contains the hash of the Git commit that was used to build the Docker image. Due to space constraints, only the section related to the Docker build is highlighted here; the whole code can be seen in the exercise on the GitHub repo.

```
docker-build:
  timeout-minutes: 10
  runs-on: ubuntu-latest
  needs: lint

  steps:
  - name: Checkout
    uses: actions/checkout@v1

  - name: Build Docker Image
    run: |
      cd source-code/chapter-7/exercise-2/newsbot-compose
      docker build -t newsbot:${GITHUB_SHA} .
```

Save this section to the workflow file, commit it, and push the changes to the GitHub repo. This should once again trigger the GitHub workflow. Examine the recent runs using the following command:

```
STATUS   NAME                 WORKFLOW              EVENT ID
✓        <commit message>  Lint and build Docker <run id>
✓        <commit message>  Lint and build Docker <run id>
X        <commit message>  Lint and build Docker <run id>
✓        <commit message>  Lint and build Docker <run id>
```

Look at the last run using the following command:

```
gh run view <run id>
```

```
✓ add-lint-build-workflow Lint and build Docker · <run id>
Triggered via push about 20 hours ago
```

```
JOBS
✓ lint in 11s (ID <job id>)
✓ docker-build in 2m57s (ID <job id>)
```

You can see that the Docker build job was also successful. You can examine the full job logs using the following command:

```
gh run view --log --job=<job id>
```

The logs are shown in Listing 8-6.

Listing 8-6. The Full Job Logs

```
docker-build    Set up job Current runner version: '2.280.3'
docker-build    Set up job ##[group]Operating System
docker-build    Set up job Ubuntu
docker-build    Set up job 20.04.2
docker-build    Set up job LTS

...

docker-build    Build Docker Image Step 7/7 : CMD ["python",
"newsbot.py"]
docker-build    Build Docker Image ---> Running in 6f3911bd1009
docker-build    Build Docker Image Removing intermediate container
                6f3911bd1009
docker-build    Build Docker Image ---> ab0d26e8298e
docker-build    Build Docker Image Successfully built ab0d26e8298e
docker-build    Build Docker Image Successfully tagged
newsbot:639bc2
```

To complete the exercise, add a final step to push the newly built Docker image to the Docker Hub. Before you can do this, you have to create an account on https://hub.docker.com. Make a note of the username and password that was used to the register—you'll be using it to authenticate with the GitHub Action. To push to your Docker Hub repository, you have to make two changes:

1. Prefix your Docker Hub username to the image in the build step.

2. Add the Docker Hub credentials to GitHub.

To add the Docker Hub credentials, from the GitHub repository where you are pushing the changes, choose Settings, Secrets. Click New Repository Secret, add DOCKER_USERNAME as the name, and enter your Docker Hub username. Repeat the same process for the password, with the name DOCKER_ PASSWORD and value as Docker Hub password that you used to register your account. Once both have been added, the Secrets section should look like Figure 8-1.

Figure 8-1. *Secrets configured in the GitHub repository settings*

With the credentials added to GitHub, you can now modify the job to inject these secrets. This can be done by referencing the secret name using the ${{ secrets.SecretName }} format. The docker-build section of the workflow file should now look like Listing 8-7.

Listing 8-7. docker-build Job Updated with Added Docker Hub Credentials and Push to Docker Hub

```
docker-build:
  timeout-minutes: 10
  runs-on: ubuntu-latest
  needs: lint
```

```
steps:
- name: Checkout
  uses: actions/checkout@v1

- name: Build Docker Image
  env:
    DOCKER_USERNAME: ${{ secrets.DOCKER_USERNAME }}
    DOCKER_PASSWORD: ${{ secrets.DOCKER_PASSWORD }}

  run: |
    cd source-code/chapter-7/exercise-2/newsbot-compose
    docker login -u ${DOCKER_USERNAME} -p ${DOCKER_PASSWORD}
    docker build -t ${DOCKER_USERNAME}/newsbot:${GITHUB_SHA} .
    docker push ${DOCKER_USERNAME}/newsbot:${GITHUB_SHA}
```

Now verify that the push happened successfully. As earlier, you can find the latest runs with the gh run list command:

```
gh run list
STATUS  NAME                WORKFLOW              EVENT  ID
✓        <commit message> Lint and build Docker <run id>
X        <commit message> Lint and build Docker <run id>
✓        <commit message> Lint and build Docker <run id>
```

Then find the results of the workflow using the following command:

```
 gh run view <run id>
```

```
✓ add-lint-build-workflow Lint and build Docker · <run id>
Triggered via push about 59 minutes ago
```

```
JOBS
✓ lint in 14s (ID <job id>)
✓ docker-build in 3m57s (ID <job id>)
```

And to view the results of the `docker-build` job, type the following command:

```
gh run view --job <job id>
```

```
✓ add-lint-build-workflow Lint and build Docker · 1198342464
Triggered via push about 1 hour ago
```

```
✓ docker-build in 3m57s (ID 3507041628)
    ✓ Set up job
    ✓ Checkout
    ✓ Build Docker Image
    ✓ Complete job
```

You can see from the summary that all the steps were completed successfully. To examine the logs of the job, issue the command shown here:

```
gh run view --log --job=<job id>
```

```
docker-build  Set up job Ubuntu
docker-build  Set up job 20.04.3
docker-build  Set up job LTS
[...]
docker-build  Build Docker Image Step 7/7 : CMD ["python",
"newsbot.py"]
docker-build  Build Docker Image Successfully built b65633d72071
docker-build  Build Docker Image Successfully tagged ***/newsbot
:48e085beba409747b3a87dcf918549017ae8c173
docker-build  Build Docker Image The push refers to repository
[docker.io/***/newsbot]
[...]
docker-build  Build Docker Image 54d6343a1c01: Pushed
```

You have successfully configured Continuous Integration to build the Docker Image on every push. When you look at the GitHub Actions page, it should look like Figure 8-2. You can now refer to this image and tag to deploy.

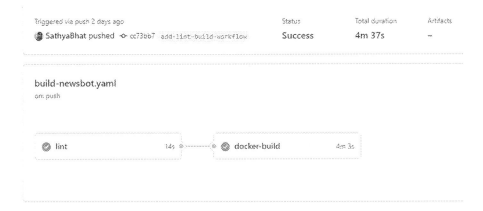

Figure 8-2. *GitHub Actions for the Newsbot lint and build*

Summary

In this chapter, you learned about Continuous Integration and how to use Continuous Integration to build Docker images automatically after every Git commit, making it easier to test containers and applications. You also learned about container orchestrators, got an overview of Kubernetes, and learned how to use kind to deploy a Kubernetes cluster on your local system to make testing your Docker applications easier and ready for production deployments. Finally, you tried some exercises on deploying a multi-node Kubernetes cluster for local development using kind and setting up a Continuous Integration pipeline that validates, lints the Newsbot source code, and then builds and publishes the Newsbot Docker image to the Docker Hub automatically on every commit, using GitHub Actions. With this, I hope you can apply the principles you learned in the book and implement similar steps in your applications!

Index

A

Actions Workflow file, 201

ADD instruction, 76, 78

Adminer container, 144

Amazon Elastic Block Store (EBS), 105

Amazon Elastic File Systems (EFS), 105

Amazon Web Services (AWS), 105

B

Bind mounts, 25, 109–114

Borg, 211

Bridge networks, 134, 135
    adminer container, 144
    containers connection, 152–155
    creation, 147–152
    host network, 155, 156
    Login with IP address, 147
    MySQL container, 142, 145

Build context, 62, 63

Build key
    context key, 176
    depends_on key, 177
    environment/env_file key, 176
    image key, 176
    ports key, 178
    volumes key, 179, 180

BuildKit
    building, Docker build, 66–69
    build output, 64
    DOCKER_BUILDKIT flag, 65
    legacy Build Process, 65
    tags, 69–71

build subcommand, 182

C

cgroups, 5

chroot, 4

Cloud providers, 105

CMD instruction, 82, 83, 85, 86

compose exec command, 182

Compose file format, 30, 169

Compose specification, 168, 171, 172, 174

Containers, 1, 4, 5, 7
    behavior, 106
    layer, 24
    runtime, 7
    volumes, 118–120

R

Replicas key, 219
Restart key, 181
RUN instruction, 79–81

S

Services key, 175
Software Defined Networking
(SDN), 134
Source code management
(SCM), 201
StatefulSet, 220
stop command, 183

T, U

Tag, 23
Telegram Messenger
BotFather
API documentation, 53
Bot creation, 51–54
options, 51
one-time password, 50
signup page, 49

tmpfs mounts, 108, 109
Typical Dockerfile, 62

V

Virtual machine (VM), 7, 15
Virtual private server (VPS), 4
VOLUME instruction, 89
Volumes, 25
container, 118–120
create, 115
inspect, 115
instruction in Dockerfiles, 121
list, 116
prune, 116
removes, 117
subcommands, 114
Volumes key, 179, 180

W, X, Y, Z

Windows Subsystem for Linux
(WSL), 15–18
WORKDIR instruction, 72–75
Worker tier, 207

Printed in the United States
by Baker & Taylor Publisher Services